PRAISE FOR WRITE ABOVE THE NOISE

"I'm constantly hearing pitches from screenwriters who are passionate about writing, but honestly, aren't very good. In most cases, they aren't good because they follow their passion instead of putting in the hard work of becoming a great writer. That's why I strongly recommend Laura Woodworth's *Write Above the Noise—Key Concepts to Develop Your Best Writing*. This is the reference every writer needs who has a story to share but needs the principles and techniques that will change people's lives. I've been writing for more than four decades, and Laura is the first person I call any time I have a question. Simply put—this book needs to be on every writer's desk."

—Phil Cooke, Ph.D.

Media Producer, Co-Founder of Cooke Media Group; Author, *Ideas on a Deadline—How to Be Creative When the Clock is Ticking*

"Laura has found the secret to exceptional writing: rely on the God of All Creativity who lives inside every Christ-follower. Her provocative questions and on-target suggestions will guide you to successfully communicate what the Spirit whispers in your heart. Superb prescriptions. Follow them and become a wonderfully effective writer!"

—Norman C. Mintle, Ph.D.

Film Producer, Blogger, Professor at ORU University

"Writing is easy; being a writer is hard. But here, Laura Woodworth breaks down the process by offering a cheerfully practical and realistic approach to writing as a craft and as an act of worship. With her own encouraging style, she examines the necessary motivations, skills, and disciplines that will help a person navigate the obstacles to starting and finishing that book, screenplay, or other work that's

been sitting there, waiting to be realized. From the blank page to the finished manuscript, the writer with Christian concerns would do well to draw from the insights found here."
—Shun Lee Fong
Filmmaker, Creative Director of The Greenhouse Arts & Media, Los Angeles; Author, *The Saints & the Poets*

"I've watched 'wannabes' come into the Hollywood entertainment industry who never seem to get it. They haven't developed the essentials or learned the fundamental steps needed to sustain a long and successful career. Laura's book is your new writing manual, and one you will want to keep on your desk and refer to again and again."
—Kathleen Cooke
Co-Founder of Cooke Media Group/Influence Women; Author, *Hope 4 Today: Stay Connected to God in a Distracted Culture*

"With deep wisdom and practical tools, Laura Woodworth guides writers to fulfill their God-given dreams. *Write Above the Noise—Key Concepts to Develop Your Best Writing* delivers a brilliant outline for aspiring creatives so they can achieve their goals. Woodworth's powerful encouragement and insights will resonate in the lives of those called to share messages with eternal meaning."
—Tina Yeager
Author, Speaker, Life Coach, Host of Flourish-Meant Podcast

"Laura is a first-class writer... What impresses me most about her is she doesn't hide her light under a bushel, nor bury her talents. She is willing to share her expertise and insights with anyone who is interested in sharing their gifts with the world. And the world needs your gifts, now more than ever. I know you will enjoy this treasure from Laura Woodworth."
—David Henriksen
President & CEO of the Giving Company

"After 15 years as a writer in the National Defense sector, Laura Woodworth's latest book, *Write Above the Noise—Key Concepts to Develop Your Best Writing* has challenged me to hone my technical as well as creative craft to a higher level.

Covering essential topics like how to develop a writing plan, find great writing content, capture your audience, and build an online presence—this Christ-exalting book is an essential resource to become the writer you have always dreamed about whether you're beginning your writing journey, or have been a prolific writer for many years. Straightforward, pulling no punches, Laura writes from the heart with a rare warmth, encouraging her readers to boldly share the unique message the Lord has placed in their own hearts with the world."

—Mahreen Shamim

Senior Compliance Analyst & Writer, Fortune 500 Company

"I don't have words to express how your words made me feel other than to say they have fueled my determination to keep 'keeping on' in this current assignment from the Lord."

—Ruby Carr

Screenwriter

"Laura's writing workshop was the release to do what I clearly heard God telling me to do—but felt so inadequate. As a first-time author, Laura's book graciously walked me through each step of the writing process. Her words of instruction and encouragement inspired me from beginning to end."

—Patty Noel

Co-founder of Her Entourage; Author, *Momistry*

"Laura Woodworth's advice while writing my first book was immeasurable. Her feedback and encouragement propelled me from struggling writer to published author."

—Heather O'Brien

Author, *Don't Let the Monsters Out: An American Airman's Descent into Darkness at Camp Bucca, Iraq* and *Chains of Freedom: Writings of a Redeemed Soul*

WRITE ABOVE THE NOISE

WRITE
ABOVE THE
NOISE

LAURA WOODWORTH

Dedicated to—

Ava Nicole, Violet Jane, Gemma Eloise, Waylon Raymond and Kyri

You give me a reason to write, a reason to share light and hope with the world.

CONTENTS

FOREWORD

C.S. Lewis laughed.

It was a Saturday evening in September 1931.

C.S. Lewis strolled with his friend, J.R.R. Tolkien through the grounds of Magdalen College on a path called Addison's Walk. The two were deeply, intensely, and meaningfully embroiled in (if you will excuse the euphemism) a "conversation" about metaphor, myth, religion, language, and literature. Tolkien was a devout Christian; Lewis was an equally "devout" atheist. The moon and the trees were the only true witnesses to these two titans of intellect and creativity grappling to come to terms with some of the most arcane issues of life.

Surprisingly, though, Lewis' laughter had not come at the expense of a joke, but rather Tolkien's belief that storytelling was, in fact, evidence of a direct and divine connection to God Himself. "We make things by the law in which we were made," Tolkien had philosophized. "We create because we are created. Creativity and imagination are God's image in us. We tell stories because God is a storyteller. *The* Storyteller."

To Lewis, this was ludicrous. However, as he laughed, a rush of wind suddenly blew on the still, warm evening and sent so many leaves pattering down the path the two men thought it was raining. Lewis' laughter turned, quite suddenly, to astonishment, and then to awe, as it seemed that God Himself, very much on cue, had decided to join the conversation.

Throughout most of human history, the Church, very much reflecting Tolkien's sentiments, led culture in artistic endeavors, from music to paintings, to writing, and drama. For centuries, it quite masterfully told stories in all forms and, as a consequence, indelibly shaped culture. However, in a tragic reversal, modern history tells the tale of The Master's Church intentionally recoiling from the arts and, in doing so, ceding its cultural influence. In fact, not only does the Church fail to shape culture, it is, sadly, being shaped *by* culture. And we, the Body, look at a world that is on fire in a thousand different ways and continue to question 'why.'

When the creations of The Creator fail to create, the world withers around them.

This is precisely why I fell in love with Laura's book.

It's not just a fantastically practical pillar of light through the desert of writing, but, most importantly, it's a spiritual call to arms. It's a reminder that *we*, the Church, are the ones who possess intimate knowledge of The Creator and should be using this privileged arcana to write the most artistic, thought-provoking, provocative, challenging, joyous, and excellent works this world hasn't seen since the likes of Lewis and Tolkien.

This isn't to say that you have to write fairy stories or even fiction. You need only to write what The Father of Lights has placed inside of your heart—be it a biography, an epic fantasy novel, a business and leadership book, a children's picture book, or a DIY book about interior design hacks. Whatever it is, it's *that* story that will impact culture. It's *that* story that will touch someone's heart or change someone's life. Why? Because if He is the one who put it in your heart, that story possesses the very DNA of God Himself.

Never, ever, ever, ever minimize the power of that truth.

Michelangelo once said, "In every block of marble I see a statue as plain as though it stood before me, shaped and perfect in attitude and action. I have only to hew away the rough walls that imprison the lovely apparition to reveal it to the other eyes as mine see it." With this perspective, Michelangelo didn't have to *create* the statue at all. It was already there. All he had to do is remove anything that was obscuring it.

Think about that.

If the Spirit of The Creator lives in you, that book—*your* book—is already there. Every concept, every idea, every poem, every essay, every monologue, every screenplay, every comedic plot, every Act Two turning point, every B-story, and every Broadway play you could need is already there as a supernatural byproduct of The Master being there first. You simply have to remove those things in your life that are keeping it covered. And just as a sculptor uses chisels, hammers, rasps, and bankers to ultimately realize her piece of art, the heap of best practices that Laura outlines in this book are the tools to realize yours.

And, trust me, they are more than enough.

You may not have the deepest experience, the most credits, the fanciest degree, or the best training. You may not have the most commercial concept, the wittiest dialogue, or the most emotionally resonant prose. You have to learn to be content with that because, like Michelangelo had his chisels, Joshua his jawbone, and Shamgar his oxgoad, you have everything you need to make an indelible impact on this world through your work.

The Old Testament teaches us about the various tribes of Israel marshaling their troops for war. Most tribes had tens of thousands of warriors, but the small tribe of Issachar only brought 200. Despite their small numbers, they weren't disadvantaged simply because they "understood the times in which they lived." To the world, you may *appear* disadvantaged. However, by understanding the times in which you live, you'll recognize the thousands of mediums, platforms, outlets, and tools available to help you tell your story. And when that happens, the perceived deficits will disappear.

It's remarkable. Out of all of human history, The Great Storyteller decided to have you live in the most advantageous, opportunistic time to tell stories since the invention of the printing press, and possibly *ever*. He could have placed you in the Dark Ages. He could have had you live during pioneer times. He could have had you in the analog 1950s. But He didn't. He not only put you here—now—with a story in your heart, but He has also given you the means to tell it.

Selah.

The stroll C.S. Lewis took on Addison's Walk that September evening opened his eyes to not only his divine call to write but also to the divine nature of writing itself. My encouragement to you is to have this book be *your* Addison's Walk. Tolkien implored us to "create because we are created." More importantly, the 78th Psalm calls us to "...open [our] mouths and tell stories."

We are charged to *fill the world* with our stories and now, with the book you hold in your hands, you can not only tell those stories, but you can tell them well.

Houston Howard
You're Gonna Need a Bigger Story

INTRODUCTION—WHY YOU SHOULD WRITE

BECOME THE WRITER YOU WERE ALWAYS MEANT TO BE

"Has the Lord redeemed you? Then speak out! Tell others
he has saved you from your enemies."
Psalm 107:1-2 NLT

Why write? Why take the time and energy to write a book, a blog or a novel? For that matter, why write and produce a film or TV show? Why do anything—unless it is for the Lord?

I believe that if you're holding this book in your hand, you have a book inside you that's waiting to come out... a story for a television series that's been keeping you awake at night... a challenging or life-changing experience you've lived through that you know would help someone else who's facing a similar situation—if you could only get it down on paper.

Having lived and worked in Los Angeles for several years, my spirit is troubled to see how the dark side of Hollywood often dictates cultural norms for the U.S. and in nations around the world. It's spurred me to write more—to wield the sword of God's word through writing that pierces the darkness with light.

And, it's created a greater desire to rally my brothers and sisters in the faith to step up with your writing projects. We need your voice. We need your words of light to shine forth and bring hope to a dying world.

Words Have Power

Words bring life or they can bring death. Blessing or cursing. Hope or destruction. More than ever before, this is a critical time to write intentionally and effectively to impact this world with life.

Developed initially as a college-level course, *Write Above the Noise—Key Concepts to Develop Your Best Writing* will arm you with the foundational writing concepts that apply to whatever medium or platform you are writing for. Whether you're a novice writer working on your first book or a veteran writer wanting to write better and faster, this book offers developmental principles that will help you write more intentionally—with the end goal of effectively engaging audiences with your writing.

This book is not a creative writing course, but it will help both fiction and nonfiction writers. While the first edition trained college students to write well as they ventured into the real world of ministry and business, this edition appeals to writers in all seasons of life who want to make a difference in the world with their faith.

Don't be fooled by the simplicity of this book; I use these same principles every day in my work as a professional writer. My screenplays have been produced, and I've consulted multiple screenwriters on their scripts. My press releases have been picked up nationally. My blogs and articles have been carried by Family Christian, iDisciple, Outreach Magazine, Charisma's Spirit-Led Woman, Pure Flix Insider, and more. My devotional plans on YouVersion's Bible app have above-average ratings and over 220,000 subscribers. My writing is finding and engaging audiences!

I'm a living testimony of what happens when you make yourself available to God and vulnerable to readers. The more I write, the more doors open for me—and they will open for you too!

If you apply these proven concepts to your writing, getting your thoughts down on paper or into a Word doc or Final Draft script template will become easier and easier! This book is your roadmap to developing stellar content that will help you become the writer you've always dreamed about or fulfill the calling you've never pursued—*until now.*

Writing is a Discipline

You can do this! You can learn to write effectively along with the hundreds of others who have relied upon this book or sat in my writing classes to achieve success in their realms of writing.

If God has saved you, speak out. Tell the world. Your book or blog or article could be the turning point in someone's life, the saving grace that inspires them to choose life or the map that helps them find their way back home to the Father who loves them.

What's Your Vision?

I hope that both your purpose and your writing will spring forth from the deep places of your spirit connected to the deep places of God—inspired by a special place in your life where earth and heaven meet.

To gain the most from this book, consider the scriptures I include with each chapter. Use these to cultivate an experience with God in your own life, to fuel the connection that will enable you to be an inspired and anointed writer.

Also, I've added writing exercises at the end of each chapter. Don't skip over those; they are designed to help you practically apply each chapter's concept. Trust the process and let them spark your journey towards starting and *completing* the writing project God has put on your heart... and the next and the next!

One final note before you begin... My writing stems from my relationship with God. He is my Source. He is my wellspring.

Without God and his word, I am nothing. I have nothing to share.

With him, I can save the world. And you can too.

I pray courage, determination and the best of success for you. As a son or daughter of God, may you rise up to bring hope and light through your writing. The world needs you.

—Laura Woodworth

1

What's Holding You Back

And How You Can Move Past It

"For the anxious longing of the creation waits eagerly
for the revealing of the sons of God."
Romans 8:19 NASB

How many books do you have inside you, waiting to be written? How many uncompleted drafts are sitting on your desk or in a file on your computer? My friend, those words will never touch a soul until you complete them and get them out for the world to read.

Growing up, my sister was the writer. I was the dancer; I was the actor. Yes, I could write, but I always pushed the deadlines and hastily scribbled my assignments at the last minute. Instead of writing a term paper for my college biology class, my classmates (cronies from the theatre department) and I wrote a script covering the required scientific topics. We then produced it as a dramatized radio show and turned in the taped recording for our final grade. (Unbelievably, I passed that class!)

The point is, I avoided writing.

That is until I encountered God in a powerful and personal way. The experience completely changed the trajectory of my life. As I grew in God, married and raised a family, I realized I had something to say.

I had a testimony and a growing knowledge of God and his word. As I learned to trust him, through the ins and outs and ups and downs of life, I realized there might be someone else who could benefit from what I'd learned. Someone who needed to know what I knew—the height, width and depth of God's love.

And then, writing opportunities came, simply from my desire to help others know God and inspire them to live for him. My daily journaling was a start, then a missionary prayer book and a Christmas play that I directed and produced with the help of my husband and kids with a cast of over 80 people. The more I wrote, the more I learned how to express what was in my heart in ways others could grasp and benefit from.

I was tagged to ghostwrite a book, which opened more opportunities until I was writing the online content for a major ministry, managing all communications through blogs and articles and press releases, developing books and study guides for print publication, and even writing on a TV show.

And now, I've finally owned up to being a writer.

Which brings me back to you. What's holding you back? In just a few short chapters, I will share my writing secrets to help you develop anything, anywhere, anytime. But first, we've got to get you writing! Let's examine the most common reasons people don't write or don't finish, even when they're passionate about a project—even when they feel God has called them to write!

WHAT'S HOLDING YOU BACK FROM WRITING?

I'm Too Busy to Write

I get it. Life is busy. *Your* life is busy. It may seem impossible to carve out even 15 minutes to complete a thought before the kids need you or it's time to start your "day job" that pays the bills. It's frustrating, especially if you sense a calling to write.

In the next chapter, we'll talk about ways to find time to write. But for the moment, I invite you to focus on why you're frustrated: the simple nagging feeling that you *should* be writing. Lean into that and you'll start finding ways to get your thoughts on paper.

A thought for a blog scribbled on a scrap of paper, a voice text to yourself of a movie idea. If you open yourself up to the inner conviction that you *should* be writing, the story ideas and concepts will come, and with them, the creative ways to carve out time to write them down.

Trust me on this. If you want to move past your obstacles, you've got to own the feeling that pokes at you that you *should* be a writer.

Who Am I To Write?
Sometimes we sabotage ourselves by allowing the "who am I" thoughts to run free in our minds. You're stalled in your tracks by intimidating thoughts that like to rattle your cage, like "Who am I to start a blog?" or "What do I have to say that can change a life?" In the industry, it's called the imposter syndrome, and it's more common than you think.

You may struggle with the thought that there's already a glut of books on your topic of expertise. "What do I have to say that's not already been said?"

Let me reassure you. Your book or blog can be unique. It can stand out above the others. Most importantly, if you are a Christian believer, you write from a unique worldview. Your book may not lend towards sharing scripture, but trust me, the light within you will shine no matter what you pen.

And of course, there are always the age-old taunts of your past or present that will do their best to hold you back and pull you under. "Your life isn't perfect. Who do you think you are?"

Your life may be messy (whose isn't?) but out of the mess can come a message. What have you gained through the trials?

God never told anyone in the Bible to wait until their life was perfect before telling a soul about him. Jesus didn't put parameters on his command to "go and make disciples of all the nations" (Matthew 28:19).

Wrestle this out and let God win in your life. You have something to say. Write it down. That simple step moves you from a frustrated dreamer to a bona fide writer.

I Don't Know Where to Start

Maybe the thought of publishing scares you. It can be daunting, but you've already taken the first step by picking up this book. The next step is to begin writing, which I'll help you with as well.

Then, when you're ready to publish, post or print, plenty of resources can help you find your way. Again, it all rolls back to getting the manuscript written.

We live in a digital age of opportunity. Anyone with a computer or a phone can reach the world with a blog post, a Twitter feed or a TikTok video. You hold the world in your hand.

The same is true of the self-publishing world. Anyone with a bit of money and a following can publish and market their book. Gone are the days of rejection letters from major publishing houses.

If you want to share your words with the world in book form, it's entirely possible as long as you're willing to self-finance if need be (at least to start) and do the research towards a successful launch.

The world is waiting for your words. All creation groans for light to be revealed in the earth.

If you have a relationship with God, you have a role to play in covering the earth with his glory—in helping your neighbor, your community or the online world know about the marvelous LIFE they can have in him.

Now that we've uncovered what may be holding you back from writing, let's see if I can inspire you to move past the roadblocks and on to your writing career.

HOW TO MOVE PAST YOUR ROADBLOCKS

If You Don't Speak Up, Who Will?

Even as there was a race to the moon in decades past, there is now an online race to gain an audience before the other guy gets there. The Hollywood Reporter (a Hollywood trade magazine) recently reported that Amazon, Netflix and Disney were racing to see who could secure the most subscribers in India, the world's biggest emerging digital economy. Somebody's going to win that country over to their service, their worldview and ultimately their agenda.

I'm not out to bash Hollywood, but our naivete blinds us if we don't recognize the agenda driving many of the films greenlighted for production or the television pilots ordered to series. Content that promotes anti-God lifestyles and worldviews abound. And in case you're not aware, even content that is scripturally based is often written by non-believers who bring their biases into the subject matter.

As a Christ-follower, this unsettles me. Coming from a missions and full-time ministry background, coupled with a fierce desire to know God and help others know him in an authentic way, my soul groans within me as I cry out, "Where are God's people in all this? Where are the ones called to spread salt and light in the earth?"

Where are the Christian writers who can write films, television, books and blogs with brilliance and inspiration? Where are the ones who will take their God-given voice to reach the nations in this digital age of opportunity and counteract darkness with light?

Is It You?

If you're holding this book in your hands, then tag—you're it! You may not feel you are the best person to write, but you can acquire and hone the skill. There will always be incredibly gifted, seemingly natural-born writers in this world, but if you're not one of them, be assured that with passion, practice and dedication (and perhaps a little help from an editing friend), you can touch lives with your writing.

The world is open to you. This book will help you envision the audience you want to share your words with and then help you develop your writing so that it is engaging and effective.

Are you ready? Let's start by identifying your passion and then identify what's holding you back. Be prepared for God to speak. He will help you find your way through to words on the paper and a published book in your hand.

EXERCISES

1. What are you most passionate about?

2. If you could write a book about anything in the world, what would you write?

3. What holds you back from writing? (Even as you answer this question, be open to and write down any creative ideas about how you can move past these hindrances.)

If you've got a screenplay or a novel burning in your soul, congratulations. You've now taken the first step towards finally writing it. In the next chapter, you'll discover how to develop the disciplines of a writer. I'll share easy steps to help you become the writer that can impact the world with your faith.

2

DEVELOP THE DISCIPLINES OF A WRITER

START THINKING LIKE A WRITER

"Commit to the LORD whatever you do, and he will establish your plans."
Proverbs 16:3 NIV

Did you discover something about yourself in the first chapter? It's amazing the things that will hold us back from writing even when we feel strongly that God is calling us to write.

Now that you've identified your roadblocks, you can move past them and get down to business. Hopefully you're beginning to own the concept of being a writer. It took me some time, but if you're sensing the nudge of God to write, I can tell you from experience that it's better to own it than avoid it!

If you haven't answered the questions in Chapter 1, I highly encourage you to take action. Take the time now to go back and identify your passion for writing and what's been holding you back from starting or completing a writing project. Allow yourself the time to gain some self-awareness at this point. Be honest with yourself and with God so you can follow through with what's on your heart.

If you've ever watched the classic movie "You Can't Take it With You," the lead character's mother is busily typing away, writing a novel. Why? Because a typewriter was accidentally delivered to their house!

Sometimes I have to pinch myself as a reminder of the wonderful realization that I've moved beyond "accidental" writing to a professional writing career.

I think the real turning point came for me when my husband gifted me my very first Macbook. I'd been dabbling with writing on a computer that I toted back and forth to work, but it sealed the deal for me when he put this tool into my hand. His support helped me dream and press forward with the writing ideas I truly felt God had placed in my heart.

I pray you have someone in your life who believes in you like that. If you don't, then consider my words as your friendly support. I believe in you. You can do this. Let your inner conviction of this calling from God guide you.

In this chapter, you'll discover the habits that will develop you as a writer. Then, you'll find out how to develop the kind of writing others will want to read.

WRITING IS A DISCIPLINE

Writing can be a wildly creative adventure, but it's also a discipline. It's a way to think and live that enables you to give in to those creative urges and divinely inspired ideas and share them with others.

It may be a special gift or talent for some, but if God has laid something on your heart to write, let me encourage you. It is a skill you can acquire.

You can discipline yourself *and* you can become a good writer!

If you have a message to share, it's worth the time and effort to become good at what you've been called to do. In this digital age, if you hone your writing skill and get savvy at your chosen genre or medium, you can reach the masses of people who are online right now.

Apply a disciplined mindset and you'll never get stuck with writer's block. You won't need to wait until you're "in the mood" to write, frustrated and accomplishing little toward your goal.

Let's break the process down.

4 DISCIPLINES TO BECOMING A GREAT WRITER

There are four keys to becoming a great writer:

1. Think like a writer.

2. Read good writing.

3. Discipline yourself to write daily.

4. Ruthlessly edit your material.

1. THINK LIKE A WRITER

People often approach me about the book or screenplay they will write "someday." Often they tell me God has called them to this task. The question that rolls through my mind is when? When are you going to start working towards that goal? Have you set a deadline? How will you start?

Your first step is to begin thinking like a writer. Writers—write! They have a plan and a place to write. They make writing a priority in their lives and gather the tools that will help them accomplish their goal. They move past the talk, put their backsides to a chair, and write.

Do you have a plan? Do you have a set-apart place where creative juices can flow and you can write freely without distraction or interference? Do you have the proper tools?

Does it seem like I'm asking too many questions? Relax. Let's explore what you, the writer, can do to set yourself up for success.

Create Your Writing Place
As a writer, it's essential to create a place to work. It may be your kitchen table or an in-home office, or you may write best with the background noise of a coffee

shop. Clean out a closet if you need to but take steps to establish your writing space.

I have a professional home office where I do my serious writing, but often, I start my brainstorming process sitting at the kitchen table. Nothing fancy, just me, a cup of tea, and a quiet place.

- **Where is the best place for you to write?** Where do you feel the most creative?

Gather Your Writing Tools

Now that you have a place to write, it's time to gather the tools for writing. My experience is that good writing begins with pen and paper.

Although you may be tempted to fire up your computer and start typing when an idea comes to you, read the research and you'll find your brain processes things differently when you work on a computer versus penning it in a notebook. I always start my writing process on paper and *then* transfer over to my laptop once I know where I'm going with my writing project. (*This* is where the Macbook my husband gave me comes into the process!)

- **Do you have a notebook and pen?** That's all you need to start.

Don't feel like you need to own a personal computer to start. My basic writing arsenal includes yellow legal pads for brainstorming, 3x5 cards to jot notes and ideas, good writing pens in black and red (more about this red pen later) and my laptop. If you don't have a home computer, don't let that be an excuse not to write. Most local libraries have computers for public use.

You don't need fancy software on your computer, but I have fellow writers who use Scrivener and Grammarly. I work in Word for most of my writing projects and Final Draft for any screenwriting. (Check out LauraWoodworth.com/writing-resources for helpful writing resources and affiliate links to Grammarly and Final Draft.)

My final note on tools: a printer is essential for a writer. We'll discuss this more later, but if possible, get a home printer. Or, print at the library or a friend's. Trust me—your writing will be elevated because you take the extra steps to print and review your words on paper.

Determine Your Best Time to Write

As you gather your tools, take a moment to determine your best time to write. My best writing happens in the morning—but that luxury is not always possible with the pressures of life and other work projects.

Some people write best in the morning, while others write best at night. Your day job or family responsibilities may dictate your writing schedule. Don't allow that to limit you or become your excuse. If it's in your heart to write, you will find a way and God's grace will be sufficient to help you work around the busyness of life.

I have learned—and you can too—to write even when I don't feel "inspired" or after a long and full day of other work. However, if possible, find your best time to write and then schedule it in your day as your writing time.

- **What's your best time to write?** Early morning? Late at night?

Deadlines Can Help

A meme is circulating about a person who's been asked how long it took them to write their script. "84 years," croaked the old woman.

Don't let that be you! Deadlines are important and they can help keep you moving toward your vision.

If you don't have a deadline imposed on you, set one yourself. Be realistic, put it on your calendar and do your best to meet the goal. Just as important, make sure to celebrate when you hit that deadline.

The publishing industry—and the film and television industry if you're tackling a feature screenplay or TV pilot—can be a roller coaster ride. To maintain your drive and optimism (and sanity), it's essential to celebrate the large and small victories.

Blog posted? Celebrate! First draft completed? Celebrate. Book deal signed? Find a way to mark the moment.

Even if it's just a smaller increment like writing every day for a week, reward yourself or at the very least share the good news with a friend. Hitting deadlines is a big deal in the publishing industry. As a writer, you'll be ahead of the game if you've disciplined yourself to meet them.

(Want more on deadlines? Especially as you turn pro with your writing, you'll appreciate this book by media executive Phil Cooke, *Ideas on a Deadline—How to Be Creative When the Clock is Ticking*.)

Remember, writers write. Begin to think like a writer and your writing project will come to fruition. Determine your best time and place, gather your writing tools and WRITE.

2. READ GOOD WRITING

Reading good writing is one of the best ways to expand your writing style and vocabulary while developing your unique voice. Top on the list is the Bible. God's word is my source, my place from which all my creativity flows! Considered a significant literary work by secular and Christian scholars, it will give you inspiration beyond yourself from which to write. (And, it provides good content. See Chapter 4.)

Move on to the classics and find good examples of your chosen genre. Read the best-sellers if you dream of writing a novel or non-fiction work. Find an author you like and figure out what makes people want to read their stuff.

Case in point, when I began writing my first thriller novel, I ended up with a stack of books from the top thriller novelists and the up-and-coming ones. David Baldacci, Noah Hawley, Terri Blackstock, Ted Dekker. I read them all, gleaning from their styles and writing techniques. It was a towering stack, but the genre was new to me and I needed to see what worked, what I liked about each author's style and what I might do differently in my novel.

If you're an aspiring screenwriter, then read scripts! Even the accomplished writers make a practice of reading the old classics as well as the new Academy Award-winning screenplays. I talk about this more in the chapter on screenwriting, but it amazes me when I consult on a script and find out the writer is not reading screenplays.

Are you a blogger? Choose a popular blogger to follow. Are you writing web content for a ministry or non-profit or business? Spend time perusing web content on other well-done websites. If you're writing and developing content for social media, see what's working on popular social media pages.

Serious Writers Do This
If you're serious about writing (and if you've gotten thus far in this book), then take the time to find out what is considered good writing in today's marketplace. What's selling? What's getting published or produced? What's finding an audience?

Recently, a friend felt compelled to write a book about her life story and contacted me for an editorial consultation. She had lived an interesting life and believed the telling of it could help others find their way through difficult times.

I gave her two suggestions. The first was to visit a local or online bookstore to research the best-selling autobiographies. The second was to read a few specific titles I felt might inspire the best way to tell her story. She followed through and now she's on the second draft of her book, far surpassing many people who are dreaming of writing... someday.

(For an update on her story and inspiration for why you shouldn't wait any longer to write your story, visit my blog and read "What's Your Story?" at LauraWood worth.com/blog/whats-your-story)

The bottom line is that you must read good writing to become a better writer. As you do, process what you like about the work and why. Pay attention to how the author engages the reader, particularly as it applies to the genre or tone you aspire to.

Writers write—and they also read.

Are you getting the hang of this? On to discipline number three...

3. DISCIPLINE YOURSELF TO WRITE DAILY

This means every single day. And preferably on your current project. I've found that the further removed I get from a screenplay or book project, the harder it is to pick it back up. Stay in the story or content and push through that first draft... and the next... and the next.

It's as if you are an athlete in training: daily writing strengthens your writing muscles. It takes determination, discipline and vision, just like an athlete training for the Olympics.

It's much too easy to do other things, thinking you'll knock them out quickly and *then* work on your book. But I've heard it said that not all activity is action. I'm constantly checking myself to make sure I don't get caught up in "activity" while avoiding the primary "action" of writing the book, the article or the script that I know I should be working on.

Tackling Big Projects

This can be especially true if you've got a big project on your plate (or on your heart!) and little time to write. You may be working a full-time job, raising a family, or volunteering somewhere, and your writing time is minimal.

How do you eat an elephant? One bite at a time.

A big project is no different. Even if it's 15 minutes or an hour, discipline yourself to set aside that time every day and write. Eventually, the time adds up and you'll soon have a finished draft in your hand.

Some writers find it helpful to mark off writing days on a calendar. This visual can boost your morale as you see how long you can maintain a writing streak. Even if no one else fully grasps the significance *yet*, acknowledge your writing accomplishments. Fill a whole month and find a way to reward yourself for the achievement.

What Else Can You Write?
Writing daily can also mean opening yourself up to other forms of writing. Keep a journal, write a blog, write a song or a poem or a letter... write every day and write your best. Don't cut corners or get lazy with your style simply because it may be for your eyes only.

Practice writing well at every opportunity. This daily practice will develop you as a writer while you work toward the more significant writing projects on your radar.

Writer Beware!
Here's a word to the wise as you develop your skills: as I mentioned earlier, your brain processes differently when working online versus working with a printed page, or with your pen and notebook in hand.

Often referred to as left-brain thinking and right-brain thinking, the left brain is responsible for logical and analytical thinking. Your right brain is where all the creativity happens. Good writing incorporates both sides of the brain but begins with right-brain thinking.

That's where you take the time to brainstorm ideas and let creative intuition rule. You need this relaxed thinking to do what top writers do: create something that no one else can.

If you open your emails or log on to Facebook, immediately your left-brain thinking takes over. You start forming a response email or composing your next Facebook post in your head.

If you intended to write, you've just stifled true creativity. You'll need that left-brain thinking later for the thoughtful organization of chapters of a book, researching printing prices and developing a marketing strategy for your first novel, but for now, close the emails, stay off the internet and set aside this time to let your right-brain dream and create.

This applies to any writing, whether your task is to pen an article or press release, a blog or a screenplay. Even writing social media posts must initially incorporate the intuitive energy of your right brain. As you establish the discipline to write, also consider ways to protect the creative process.

You've established three new disciplines to propel you to becoming a writer! Now let's look at one more discipline that will help you achieve your writing goals.

4. RUTHLESSLY EDIT YOUR MATERIAL

Remember that red pen in your writing arsenal? Here's where you wield it! But first, one caveat before you attack the page with red marks.

Allow yourself to write your first draft freely and without judgment. Spit out that first draft *without* your critiquing cap on. *Then* pick up your red pen for the next pass, your second draft.

One of the most challenging skills for novice and even seasoned writers is the ability to ruthlessly edit your own material. We quickly see the shortcomings in another's writing, but we cling like crazy to our pet phrases or "perfect" sentences.

Your red pen is your friend as you cross out, move or slash words on the page. To be a good writer, you must be willing to "kill your darlings." The favorite sentence you're unwilling to trim is probably the sentence holding you back from stellar writing.

The editing continues when you've transferred your work over to your computer. Don't be afraid to press delete. I dare you. See what happens to your writing when you're willing to cut a line for the sake of the overall piece.

Create a Scrap Document as You Edit
During the writing process, I create a "scrap" document in my computer files

where I save these bits of writing that I cut from my main draft. I have the scrap doc open beside the main document on my computer screen as I edit.

While I shape the main body of work, cutting out words or whole sentences and even paragraphs, I paste those over to the scrap file in case I decide to pull that copy back into the main draft or for those situations where I have a great paragraph or line of dialogue but it's in the wrong place and better suited elsewhere.

I've opened a new scrap document even as I write this. You may never see the sentence I just cut from this draft. *Or maybe you will...*

Cut the Fluff

As you edit your material, develop an eagle eye for wordiness. Learn to be succinct! This applies to all types of writing, whether or not you have a word or character limit. Don't be a lazy writer. Get your red pen in hand and cross out extraneous or redundant words and phrases. In other words, cut the fluff!

Once you've whittled away the excess verbiage, push yourself to identify weak nouns, verbs, or phrases that water down your writing. Elevate your writing by using strong nouns and verbs that paint a picture for your reader.

If you feel like we just waded into a pool that's way over your head, don't stress. In Chapter 6, you'll gain more in-depth "power writing" skills to help you critically examine your work before it goes to an editor or a helpful friend. But while we're on the topic, I'll share a little-known editing secret that will instantly bump your skills up a notch.

Writing Hack to Elevate Your Writing Quickly

Here's the secret: the last sentence you're inclined to add to a piece of writing is typically the one you should leave off. Delete it and see if your article sounds better without it!

Train yourself to stop adding to your blog, book chapter or scene before weakening it. See what happens, and you'll discover that 99% of the time, this tip is true. It will elevate your work instantly.

I'm saying all this assuming that you've printed your piece for the editing process. Remember, your brain works differently when you see things on paper versus staring at those same words on a screen, so it's essential to print your work.

It's incredible the number of times I'll print out someone's bulky 500-page manuscript (or worse yet, a 200-page screenplay) for a book or screenwriting consultation, only to find out that the author has never printed their work. If you're a professional writer (or aspiring), get the tools you need to do your work well, including a printer or access to one to do your best edit.

I can't stress the importance of *ruthlessly* editing your material as you begin to think like a writer. Good writers write, read—and are brave enough to edit their material towards their best draft.

EXERCISES

1. Develop a writing plan. When is the best time *and* where is the best place for you to write? Do you need to adjust your schedule to block writing time—or move furniture to create a writing space? Write your plan out here and list what you can do to create an atmosphere for creativity.

2. Develop a reading plan. Many successful people have a goal of reading one new book every month. You can establish a reading plan targeted toward your writing goals. Start your reading list with at least three books, blogs or articles that inspire you:

    1.

    2.

3.

3. Become a disciplined writer who writes every day. Make a list of the types of writing you can incorporate into your life daily (i.e., journaling, blogging, commenting on online articles, composing Facebook posts, songwriting):

1.

2.

3.

4. Buy a red pen. Make it part of your writing arsenal as you learn to edit your material. (Smile! Take a picture with your red pen and post it on Instagram. Tag me @laurawoodworthwriter.)

5. Do you have a writing project in mind? A book or screenplay or hit song? List it here with a realistic projected deadline and include it in your disciplined writing plan.

We've covered a lot of ground in this chapter. If you seriously feel called to write, these writing disciplines will help guarantee your success. Take the steps necessary to apply these four disciplines and you'll be well on your way to becoming a real writer. Here they are again:

4 KEYS TO BECOMING A GREAT WRITER

1. Think like a writer.

2. Read good writing.

3. Discipline yourself to write daily.

4. Ruthlessly edit your material.

Incorporate these disciplines into your life, and instead of talking and dreaming about your book, soon you'll be holding a published copy in your hand.

Now let's move on to developing your best work. This next chapter will be groundbreaking for you in your writing journey.

3

Four Key Questions For Writing Development

The Secret to Great Writing

"It is God's privilege to conceal things and the king's privilege to discover them."
Proverbs 25:2 NLT

Are you beginning to think like a writer? Have you determined a writing plan and a place to do your best writing?

More than anything, I want to encourage you that your voice and what you have to say are important. People are searching for hope, searching for something—or Someone—to believe in. Your book, blog, or article with a faith perspective could be the turning point in someone's life.

My top-performing article to date was one of the quickest things I've ever written. The words flowed from the Lord to my heart and onto the page. How glad I am that I had my notebook in front of me—that I had developed the discipline of writing daily. I was prepared to write.

"Safe—The High Tower of the Lord" brought hope to tens of thousands of readers when the pandemic was raging. Ranked as the number one performing article on FamilyChristian.com, I had no idea the impact the article would have when I first penned it, sitting at my kitchen table early one morning. It's still impacting lives today.

You'll have moments like that as well. Your writing will impact lives far beyond what you can imagine. But don't miss the irony that if I hadn't been prepared with my pen and notebook, the article may never have been written and certainly would not have had the reach it attained.

Discipline yourself to think and act like a writer. Be prepared for the Lord to use you to reach multitudes with a word of encouragement or insight.

THE SECRET TO GREAT WRITING

What I'm going to share next is your pathway to becoming a great writer. This process is something I use every single time I sit down to write—no matter if it's a social media post, blog, book or screenplay. This is the secret that I employ. Every. Single. Time.

If you've ever suffered from "writer's block," this secret will knock those two small (but paralyzing) words out of your vocabulary. As mentioned before, writer's block often happens when you neglect the disciplines that characterize a great writer. It also happens to writers who fail to develop their writing.

How many times have you had an inspiration and started to write, but after twenty minutes you hit a roadblock or a brick wall? You've painted yourself into a corner and now you're at an impasse and can't write your way out. Or you've gone down so many rabbit trails that you've simply lost your way.

And so, with your trash bin overflowing with crumpled papers, you scroll your Twitter feed or check your emails—anything to forget about the deadline for the piece. Or worse, to avoid the uncomfortable feeling that you don't know how to move forward with the inspired idea you truly felt was from God.

Until you take the time to develop that great idea, almost everything you write will be fodder for the wastebasket.

Does this sound like the voice of experience? It is. Anytime I tackle a writing project without processing the development questions below, I waste time and effort. I may jot the initial idea for a new script or an article down on a scrap of paper, but I've learned that good development is critical before I flesh out the story. It ultimately speeds the writing process and lends towards better overall writing.

The old saying that "writing is rewriting" is true. *However* you can cut down your rewriting time by developing your writing before you type "FADE IN" on your screenplay or "Chapter 1" on your novel.

Ask yourself the four simple questions below and you'll be well on your way to something impactful that others will want to read. That is our intent, isn't it—for others to read our material? For someone to read your novel from cover to cover and clamor for the next one, or for a studio executive to read your screenplay in one sitting and become passionate enough to produce it. Or for your blog to be so engaging that it goes viral. A well-developed piece can do that!

In its simplest form, writing development in any genre or medium can be boiled down to four questions:

4 KEY QUESTIONS TO DEVELOP YOUR WRITING

1. What do I want to say?

2. Who do I want to say it to?

3. What medium am I writing for?

4. What is my goal or call to action?

Let's explore these further and help you apply them to your writing.

1. WHAT DO YOU WANT TO SAY?

Notice I didn't ask, "What do you want to write about?" That's a good place to begin brainstorming, but you'll be wasting time and effort if you stay there. You may want to write a blog *about* your recent trip to Israel, but you've first got to pinpoint what you really want to communicate.

What Do You Want To *Say*?

Did the trip change your life? How so? Did it make the Bible come alive to you? In what way? Was the landscape incredible or the people amazingly friendly? *What do you want to say?*

Choose one thing and explore the possibilities of how to communicate that thought.

Are you a mommy blogger? Perhaps you want to write *about* an epiphany moment with one of your kids. Maybe you had a breakthrough in relating to their learning style or understanding what motivates them to do their homework. You want to share that with your readers, but the big question is: what do you want to say?

Did it open a new dynamic in the parent-child relationship? Did it teach you to rely on God's wisdom for parenting your fifth-grader?

Determining what you want to say before putting pen to paper will elevate your writing in powerful ways.

If you have not defined or discovered this ahead of time, you will soon find yourself staring at a blank screen or wallowing around in meaningless words that don't express your heart or intent. You wanted to help and inspire other moms, yet your blog seems dry and lifeless.

Until you have determined what you want to say, your work will never hit the mark and will remain at that level of writing "about" your summer vacation you wrote in grade school. It may be nice writing—but not developed into a piece that a magazine would carry or a publisher would print.

Brainstorm the Possibilities

Sometimes we really don't know *what* we want to say when we start writing. There have been instances when I've been given a topic for a writing assignment, but the producer or organization has left it up to me to flesh out the article.

Before I start writing, I'll take out a pad of paper and brainstorm to explore the possibilities or slants I could take on that subject. I may research online to learn more about the topic or see what others have written about it. I usually incorporate keyword research in this discovery phase to find out the questions people are asking about my topic. (We'll discuss keyword research in a later chapter.)

Brainstorming doesn't have to be a long, drawn-out process, although it will be for some projects, depending on the topic and length of the piece. But it is vital to explore your topic to determine what you want to express.

If you're our mommy blogger, you want to communicate something meaningful and relevant to your audience. You've just had that epiphany with your child, and before you write *about* it, fill a paper will all the ways to share the moment with your readers. Consider all the angles and important points or lessons. Then start honing in on what would be most impactful, interesting and relevant to your audience. This discovery process will help you decide what you want to *say* about the moment.

Narrow it Down

After you've brainstormed and done the necessary research on your topic, now narrow in and choose one focus, one thing to communicate. Too often, we try to say it all in one shot.

Have you ever read an article that covers so many topics it becomes overwhelming? I have. Those are the articles I save to read later when I have more time (a.k.a. never) or delete because it's too much to pick through to find the "nuggets" that prompted me to read them in the first place.

Also, if you want to write for the masses, think beyond your own interests as you brainstorm and determine what you want to say. Create marketing appeal by writing on the topics that interest you *and* your target audience, the "avatar" that personifies whom you are writing for.

For example, perhaps you want to write a book about gardening. Congratulations. You will be competing with the other 101,859 books on gardening I found on Amazon today. (See what I did there? I took 30 seconds and googled it.)

When you have such a broad topic, my advice is to find a way to take your topic and spin it so it becomes fresh and relevant. For your book to rise to the top, it may mean considering which audience is the best to target. For example, if you're keen on gardening, consider targeting millennials with a book about *urban* gardening or how to grow a garden within the confines of an apartment balcony.

What do you want to say to this audience? "Even if you only have a small balcony, you can grow a thriving garden."

That book will have a much better chance of being found and read than the broad topic of a book about gardening. Notice how the topic was chosen and then narrowed with the audience in mind. We'll talk more about this in just a moment.

Let Passion and Expertise Inform Your Decision

Often we hit upon a topic that offers several ways to spin it that are all equally intriguing and marketable. That's where it's critical to let your passion and expertise inform your decision as you develop a piece.

A friend approached me recently with a desire to write a book about prayer. She was a special ed teacher, so I knew she had a wealth of experience dealing with parents and children with special needs. Instead of competing with the zillion other books on prayer or the big-hitters in ministry like Lisa Bevere and Joyce Meyer, I posed this challenge: Can you spin your prayer topic to offer help and hope to the parents of special needs kids? I've seen her rough draft and I think she's grabbed a niche with her revised focus.

What do *you* want to say? Consider what qualities, passion, and experience you bring to the table to make the topic unique while creating a marketable piece that will find an audience.

This narrowing and defining of your focus will strengthen your writing. Parameters can be good for keeping your writing on track and keeping your readers engaged with you on the journey.

Now let's move on to development question number two. We've already touched on it a bit, as it goes hand in hand with considering what you want to say...

2. WHO DO YOU WANT TO SAY IT TO?

Determining your audience now will affect the slant or "hook" of your writing. Just as we read about my friend slanting her book on prayer to speak to parents with special needs kids, good writing development includes deciding who you want to reach.

Who are you writing for? To whom is this message or teaching or inspirational thought best suited? If you were to create an avatar for this person, what would he or she look like?

Are you writing for other moms? Do you hope to reach millennials, GenZs or the Boomer generation? Women, men or a mixed demographic? Who is your "target audience" that you are honing this message for? *Who* do you want to say it to?

Obviously, you will write differently towards seniors than you would towards GenZs, the same as you might write differently if your book or blog is geared towards brand new believers in Christ than those who are well-established in the faith. A book written to help young adults live out their faith will be penned uniquely if you're writing for a Muslim background believer with their uncommon challenges rather than the "typical" American young adult.

Know Your Audience

When I'm invited to write an article or devotional, one of my first questions for the editor or brand manager is: "Who is your audience?"

I'll also ask if their readership is a mix of male and female or skewed to one or the other, and what are their ages. This all comes to bear on how I develop the piece.

Keep the faces of these people—your target audience—in front of you while writing and you will be more effective in accomplishing your purpose.

Also, be aware that there may be times you will create more than one version of the same piece with the intent to target different audiences. A classic that comes to mind is the book "In His Steps" by Charles Sheldon and the children's adaptation titled "What Would Jesus Do?" Same story, same "what do I want to say" for the storyline, but as the readership changed, so did the writing to best connect with the varied age groups.

Another easy example would be a press release. Maybe you're ready to write a press release announcing your new book. You'll need two drafts if you're planning both a national and local release to media outlets: one geared for a national audience, and another version slanted towards your local community with their unique interests and including your tie-in to the locale.

As you develop every writing project, the first two questions in your mind should always be—

"What do I want to say *and* who do I want to say it to?"

Tailor your work accordingly.

Are you still with me? Before continuing, remember that, as a professional writer, I work through these development questions every time I write. They may sound incredibly simple and basic, but they really are the key to nixing writer's block and elevating your work while writing intentionally towards a specific audience.

Now let's look at two more essential questions you must ask as you develop your work.

(And don't worry, you'll have opportunity to put these into practice at the end of this chapter to help you gain a solid understanding of writing development. Then, coming up in Chapter 8, we'll delve into conducting keyword research to help you target a specific audience or need.)

3. WHAT MEDIUM ARE YOU WRITING FOR?

Now that you've thought through what you want to say and who you want to say it to, we need to look at the type of medium you will be writing for. Where will this piece live?

Is it for a hardbound book you can hold in your hand? A blog post? A print magazine or online magazine? Social media post? A print letter sent by snail mail or an online email campaign? Film, television, or new media? The medium you choose will determine your tone, writing style, structure, word choice and even the length of your piece.

There are unique differences between an article written for a print magazine versus an online version of a similar article. A Twitter post calls for a different style than a Facebook post. If you're a nonprofit or writing for one, an email campaign to your donors will be written much differently than a print letter for a direct mail campaign.

For example, a mommy blog will take on a different tone than an article for Parents Magazine. The blog style may be informal and light, with right-brain, easy-to-read, easy-to-skim words and silly stories of the things your kids say and do. The print magazine article may incorporate a more formal tone with "bigger" left-brain words and might even include statistics or data to help back up your topic.

It's interesting to note that The Wall Street Journal is reportedly written at an 8th-grade level. And current research shows the best-performing blogs are written at a 5th-grade level.

If you're writing for a visual medium such as film or television, even then you have to answer the question of your intended result. Where is this project going to live and be watched? Will it be viewed on the big screen with a theatrical release or produced for the small screens of a smartphone? Streaming platform or network television? The medium matters and will guide your writing choices.

The bottom line for all types of writing is that you've got to know and utilize the proper writing skills for the particular medium.

Research Current Trends

One caveat to be aware of is that mediums flux and change. That's why I'm not filling this book with specific medium guidelines. Whereas an 800-word online article would be a smash a few years ago, today you may find that a 450-word (or less) blog will engage audiences best. Mailchimp (an email marketing platform) recently revised its suggested optimal word count to only 200 words. Even the word count of novels fluctuates, and your 100,000-word novel may be better served as a 70,000-word novella—especially if you're a new author.

Go online to find out current best practices. Do your research and write for the medium your audience calls for, which brings us back to our earlier question, "Who do you want to say this to?"

Your Audience May Determine Your Medium

It bears saying that the demographics of your target audience and the purpose of your writing ("What do I want to say and who do I want to say it to?") also affect the choice of medium.

Where does your intended audience hang out? Are they reading blogs and articles online? Or do they love a print magazine like *Magnolia* published by Chip and Joanna Gaines?

It used to be that Facebook was the social media platform to be on. However, social media is ever-evolving and, as with all other mediums, you must keep up with the trends to inform your media choice. You may be better served to establish your voice on Instagram or Twitter depending on who you want to reach as audiences shift their attention and loyalties.

Another interesting trend is that although eBooks at one time were thought to replace print books, people still like to hold a print book in their hands! Print is not obsolete but rather complemented by the eBook or audiobook version of the title.

Do the research and go where your audience avatar hangs out. Then become adept in writing for that medium.

Choose the Best Medium for Your Audience and Story

I increasingly advise people who dream of writing a book to start by creating a blog. A blog requires you to craft your topic differently for the online medium than for your *hopefully* best-selling print publication, but it's a great strategy that allows you to build an audience.

Especially with new authors, publishers are more likely to sign you on if you've established a fan base, a built-in audience that will mitigate their risk. If you're self-publishing, an established audience will help your book launch. Plus, the shorter style of a blog will force you to define your voice and your message before you tackle the larger project of a book or novel.

Also, sometimes when I consult on a script, depending on the story and the intended audience, I might suggest that the screenwriter consider reworking their feature-length screenplay into a television series. It requires a different writing style and structure to write a teleplay over a screenplay, but if it better serves the story and intended audience, it's worth the time to adjust and learn the medium.

All this to say, as you determine what you want to say and who you want to say it to, you must also determine the best medium to reach your audience. What's important to remember is that the development questions you are learning in this book will enable you to become adept in *whatever* medium you choose.

Once the medium is selected, your work is to gain the skills necessary to write effectively in it. A good writer will learn the parameters and writing style that fit best for that medium or platform.

This is a key component in writing development. When you understand the expectations of the different mediums and shape your writing accordingly, the impact of your work will increase as well as your readership. I'll touch on writing styles in later chapters, but again the caveat applies that in this digital age, everything fluctuates. What works today may not work tomorrow. However, the basic concepts will still apply.

Before tackling the fourth development question, make sure you're solid on the first three. Here they are again:

1. What do I want to say?

2. Who do I want to say it to?

3. What medium am I writing for?

There's one more critical development question that will guide your development process...

4. WHAT IS YOUR GOAL OR CALL TO ACTION?

What is your intention in writing this piece? Answering this question in the development process will spare you the pain of writing something that leaves your reader wondering where you are going—and possibly preventing them from reading your next blog or article.

Some people call this your "why." In other words, what is your goal or "call to action" with this writing project? Before you begin writing, know where you're going with your piece and *why*.

Why do you want to say this? What do you want to accomplish through this body of work?

Determine the outcome now and you're much more likely to hit that mark and move people towards your goal or call to action. It's like mapping out your point A to point B. Where are you going? What do you want people to do or feel after reading your blog, singing your song, or watching your movie? Who do you want your reader to become once they've read your book?

This is especially apparent in sales writing or an email campaign where you need to have a call to action incorporated into the text such as a button to "buy now" or "find out more here." However, it's important to process this for other writing styles so you can make an impact with your writing.

What's Your Goal or Intention?

Your goal or "why" can be as simple as offering hope to the reader, or it can go even deeper to change their mindset or move them to action. For example, a well-written book can stir feelings of empathy towards a people group, raise awareness about a cause, open up a new worldview to your reader—or simply be a thoroughly enjoyable read. What is your goal or call to action?

A song can lift hearts, bring hope, or take us deeper in our relationship with God. Once produced and in movie theatres, a screenplay can powerfully impact an audience, causing them to feel stirred or their hearts warmed—or again, simply to be wonderfully entertained.

Consider the story of the beloved hymn "It Is Well with My Soul" written by Horatio Spafford, penned after losing all four of his daughters at sea. He may not have gone through a formal development of the song, but his "why" in writing the lyrics shines forth as he declares his trust in God. "Whatever my lot, Thou has taught me to say, it is well, it is well with my soul."

Why are you writing this piece? What is *your* goal or call to action?

Even a college writing assignment must have a "why" behind it beyond simply meeting the class deadline. You may have been tasked to write *about* racial injustice in America, and you've determined what you want to *say* about it and to whom – but *why* do you want to say it? What is your desired end result?

If you don't define your goal, you'll miss the mark every time and your writing will seem meaningless and wandering, and need I say it, boring.

Writing is hard work. It's up to you to define the passion behind this project.

Trust me, when you're on your second or third or fifth draft, that passion, your reason for writing, will keep you moving forward. Without it, you won't have the heart to finish. And, even if you do push through to completion, if you're missing a strong "why" to guide you, your writing will not engage with readers to the level of involvement you had hoped.

TO SUMMARIZE

We've covered a LOT of ground in this chapter. And we haven't even started writing yet!

But I guarantee you that if you make these four development questions part of your writing arsenal, you will become a writer that readers love and look to. Your work will find an audience. Lives will be enriched through your words.

Be intentional with your writing development. Ask the questions and ask them every time you sit down to write. It's a tried and tested writing discipline that will carry a novice or even a seasoned writer to become someone who can write intentionally and effectively. Envision where you want to be—or where you could be—in six months, a year, or even ten years down the line in your writing career if you elevate your skills now.

Before you begin any sort of writing, discipline yourself to work through the four development questions and to have at least a simple outline as your guide. (We'll delve into outlining in Chapter 5.)

With a plan mapped out, the writing process will be quicker, easier—and for those who have struggled with writing, much less painful! Plus, your work will be more enjoyable and engaging. Here are the four development questions again:

1. What do I want to say? (Notice this is different than what you're writing about.)

2. Who do I want to say it to? (This is your target audience.)

3. What medium am I writing for? (Print? Web? Screenplay or teleplay?)

4. What is my goal or call to action? (This is your "why.")

Now let's practically apply these to your writing...

EXERCISES

1. Write or print out the four development questions and place them in a prominent place in your writing area. On every project, copy those questions over to the top of your page and work through each to develop your writing for a stronger, more compelling piece.

2. Choose something you want to write "about" and develop it! This can be an actual writing project or a fun exercise. I suggest you limit this to a page or paragraph. Brainstorm and work through the four development questions and jot a quick outline on a separate piece of paper. Do that now—and then move on to exercise three...

3. Ready – set – write! Write a solid first draft of the topic you've just developed. (You can save this draft and work on it in later exercises if you want to elevate your writing.)

If you need an easy assignment to get your creative juices flowing, write "about" your most memorable summer vacation. Visualize it first... imagine your feet dangling off the deck on a lake in Wisconsin or the wind blowing in your hair at the top of a Ferris wheel at Disneyland.

Then determine: "What do you want to say" about that vacation? Explore beyond the simple writing "about" the great fishing or the fun rides to go deeper. Was it a defining moment in your childhood? Did it bring your family together—or tear it apart?

Next, who do you want to say it to? Your kids? Your spouse? A best friend?

Then, what medium will you write in? A postcard, a blog, an entry in your life journal, or an Instagram post with a photo dug out of your photo album?

And finally, just one more question: *Why* do you want to say it? What is your goal or call to action? Are you trying to talk your best friend into a road trip to Disneyland? Convince your kids of the value of a week at the lake *instead* of a theme park? Find the bright spot in an otherwise mishappen vacation? What's your goal or intended result?

Have fun with this exercise! Remember that asking yourself the four development questions is the best way for you to elevate your writing *quickly*. Test the process and you will be amazed at how easy it becomes to develop a writing piece.

ADDITIONAL EXERCISES

4. Do you have a book project in mind? How can you slant your topic so it will appeal to a particular audience? Apply this same concept to a blog, a Facebook post or a print article you are working on. Who are you trying to reach? What are ways you can spin your topic to reach your target audience?

5. Take that same book or writing project and consider how you could swing this to reach a different audience.

Sometimes writers struggle because they don't know what to write about or even where to start. In our next chapter, we'll explore ways to find great content so that you'll always have something to write about—your springboard to flesh out what you want to say.

4

FINDING GREAT CONTENT AND TAKING GREAT NOTES

HOW TO FIND IDEAS

"...you all must be quick to listen, slow to speak..."
James 1:19 NLT

Look at you! If you have diligently worked through the prompts for writing development—the four key development questions—you just moved to the head of the class, the front of the pack, the tip of the spear... Well, you get my point: you're ahead of the game. You've gained skills that some pro writers never fully grasp to be better, faster and more impactful with their writing.

If you skipped over the exercises, go back now and work through them. Trust me, the writing process will be so much simpler and you'll be astounded at how quickly you can develop something if you only take the time to ask these four simple but critical questions. No matter what medium, and no matter what tone— funny, smart, serious, inspirational—by implementing strong development skills, you've just raised your writing above the status quo.

Now, let's add to your writing toolbox with some tips for finding great content!

FINDING IDEAS AND DISCOVERING CONTENT

Someone recently asked me where I come up with my writing ideas. My number one source is my relationship with God. I begin every day with early morning quiet times of reading the Bible, listening for God's voice, and opening my heart and mind to his perspective on life and love and people.

As a Christian and especially as a writer, that awareness of God's presence carries over to how I live my life. I don't consistently achieve it, but I do my best to be cognizant of the world around me; to be curious and interested in people and events and the dynamics of relationships and society. To look at life from God's point of view and maintain a Christian worldview in the midst of a turbulent society.

If you want longevity in your writing career or ministry, developing this openness and curiosity is essential. Ultimately, content is king when it comes to writing.

You may be able to write a blog or two when the mood strikes you, but a mindset of observation and discovery steeped in God's word and his presence will sustain the writing necessary to maintain a blog long-term or finish your book (and move on to the next!).

Do You Know Your Audience?
We're back to talking about your audience again! Knowing what constitutes valuable content often boils down to understanding the interests and passions of your audience.

What blog topic will attract the attention of busy moms at home? What online article will grab the eyes of someone from the Boomer generation or GenZ as they scroll through their news feed?

It's essential to think through the lens of their lives.

Know your audience and write towards them—their needs and wants and sometimes unspoken desires. Let your writing offer value, inspiration, or solutions to their questions, whether articulated or not. This mindset will guide you toward the content that will resonate with your intended audience.

Having said that, let's look at ways you can discover great content—much of which is easily within your reach.

4 WAYS TO FIND GREAT CONTENT

I've determined four ways for you to discover the content that will fuel your writing:

1. WRITE FROM YOUR RELATIONSHIP WITH GOD.

Are you spending time in God's word and in his presence? As I mentioned above, this is core for me as a writer. As believers, time with God should be a pre-requisite for our lives and a bountiful place to draw new and inspired content.

Every morning, you will find me seated at my kitchen table or on my patio (or if I'm traveling, clearing a space in the hotel room) with my Bible, a pen, and an open notebook. God is my source and without his word and his inspiration, I really have nothing to say.

It's amazing what new thoughts and ideas come to me when I read my Bible—and not just for devotional or inspirational writing. There have been times when I've run into a brick wall while searching for a plot line on a screenplay or developing an article. My commitment to a dedicated time with God opens up the creative thought processes that help me rise above my finite thinking.

If you're stuck for content, seek God, pray, spend time in his word, and draw from God's presence for inspiration. In my mind, this is the key to an enduring professional writing career.

2. BE A STUDENT OF LIFE AND TAKE NOTES.

Recently, I attended a gathering that featured a speaker I admire. She talked for 20 minutes and I walked away with two pages of notes—insightful information from the POV of a woman who had a long career in the film industry. Upon looking around, I have a feeling I was one of the few taking notes, and the talk wasn't recorded.

Maybe others remember things better than I, or perhaps they soaked up the inspirational parts better by *not* taking notes. I just recognize that I learn and remember best when I jot important things down. Plus, I always have those notes to refer to—weeks or even months down the road.

Being a student of life means just that. Studying and learning and growing through every interaction, every experience you encounter. I'm always searching for new content or an opportunity to tap into a new perspective. As a writer, I carry a notebook and pen, even if it's a small notepad tucked into my purse. Or, I'll have my phone with me to type or voice text a thought or a conversation.

Are you thinking more and more like a writer? Then I encourage you to be prepared to take notes as you learn and grow and listen.

Set Yourself Up for Success

Remember when you were a kid and you would go shopping for school supplies? It's the same for you as a writer—those lazy summer days are over (if you're serious about this) and it's time to gear up!

Your "gear" may be as simple as a notebook and pen, but may include a phone app to help you capture thoughts and notes from sermons, classes, seminars, meetings, interviews, phone calls—anything that applies to the type of writing you do.

If I'm driving and a thought or a line of dialogue or description comes to me, I have a notebook in the car to scribble thoughts down, or I'll ask Siri or the Captio app to save a note or reminder for me. Voice memos are great too, and for interviews or phone calls I use TapeACall Pro (after asking permission from the interviewee).

If you're writing for a ministry or nonprofit, always listen at meetings and events to consider what could be significant, interesting, or just plain fun to share with the public. Turn a sermon into a white paper to offer on your website. Take a compliment from a call center phone call and build it into an article or press release. Ask permission to share the caller's name to validate the quote further.

I literally created a job for myself simply because I took notes. As I captured what God was doing at my church, my notes became the source for writing the ministry's web content, articles, press releases, blogs, social media posts and even books and devotionals.

3. OBSERVE THE WORLD AND PEOPLE AROUND YOU.

People do and say interesting things and their stories or experiences can help form the basis of an engaging writing piece. A good writer will always listen, observe, and glean from the world around them.

A novelist or screenwriter may pay special attention to the look, feel, and even smell of a particular setting they want to incorporate into their novel or screenplay. People-watching should be part of your arsenal for developing interesting characters.

A blogger might pay attention to the daily news or trending themes on the internet to fuel their next blog and form the basis for their comments on the world around them. Or the same observation might inspire you to write an article for a women's magazine or your next devotional piece.

Overheard conversations have found their way into the dialogue in several of my screenplays. Moments I have been unsuspectingly privy to have been burned into my memory or notated in the app on my phone and stored for future writing (obviously with discernment depending on the nature of the conversations; some things are not meant to be shared.)

I'll never forget an encounter I had on a set in Hollywood. The make-up artist had tattoos all over her body—Disneyland characters burned in dark ink on her legs, arms and torso. A limb from the talking tree Groot wound down her arm and onto her fingers.

I asked if there was significance to the tattoos and she told me the story of how, as a child, her family planned a birthday party for her at Disneyland and invited all the girls from her class. The big day came—but not one of her classmates showed up.

Since that day, her father took her to Disneyland every year on her birthday, a special outing for just the two of them. As she grew older, she started adding the tattoos as reminders of the unkindness of the world and the love of her father.

Without sharing names, her story became the springboard for a blog I wrote years later to help readers gain healing from the wounds of their pasts through the love of our Heavenly Father. (You can read the blog here: https://www.laurawoodw orth.com/blog/the-girl-with-the-disney-tattoo).

It's priceless what you can glean if you simply become aware of the people and the happenings around you.

4. RESEARCH STATS AND OTHER SOURCES TO VALIDATE YOUR TOPIC.

A good writer finds sources to support and add interest to their writing. Your source material will depend on your topic as you explore what you want to say and to whom.

Statistics, other books, and interviews with experts can lend credibility to your writing, depending on the tone, style and intent of your piece. The internet offers incredible resources at your fingertips, but you must choose your sources wisely and only use the ones you can trust. With that precaution, a few extra moments researching statistics to build into an article or news brief can increase impact.

A relevant statistic can tie the bow on your blog or lend credibility to a direct mail letter or email campaign soliciting support for your ministry's cause. One word of caution: depending on the writing project, I wouldn't necessarily lead with cold hard data. Facts don't typically move a person; stories do. Consider leading with a story and then support it with statistics.

Also, consider structured ways to gain input from people to help fuel your writing. A survey on your website or social media can easily help you gather content (and help you know your audience better). A contest that invites fans, supporters or congregants to create content becomes a new source of creative and interesting material that you can purpose *or* repurpose to share with your audience.

Research Saturation

For certain types of writing, I aim for "research saturation." Especially when writing a screenplay or book, I strive to immerse myself in my characters' topic or story world. I build that valuable research time into my writing schedule. It lends toward more believable writing.

For example, a few years ago, I was brought on to write a screenplay based on a young woman's true story of how she broke free from slave trafficking. It's a remarkable narrative of how she overcame the odds and then went on to affect change within state and federal governments so that others in similar situations would have a better chance at life.

My first source for content was the group of individuals who intimately knew my main character. I booked a number of interviews, taking notes or recording the meetings on my phone. Then, because of the nature of the story, I scoured through medical records, police records and more to gain facts and get to the heart of the story. I gathered statistics and then looked at other stories similar to hers to develop the slant I would take with this screenplay—my "what do I want to say" and "to whom."

If this sounds like a lot of work—it was. But the in-depth research allowed me to write the screenplay from a better vantage point, thus capturing the true essence of her story.

Often, beginning writers only write from their experiences. A seasoned, proactive writer goes the second mile and fills the experiential gaps with research and input from other sources. Even if you never use the research you've gained (I have 3-ring binders full of research on one screenplay, and probably used two percent of it in my writing), it has at the very least strengthened your perspective for better, more insightful work.

A brief word of caution in conducting in-depth research is to make sure you don't drown in the details. Find the story and then get busy writing. Don't let research turn into procrastination.

Are you getting the hang of this? I recently listened to an interview with John Maxwell, a prolific writer who always seems to have something valuable to say, particularly on leadership. He creates folders on different topics relevant to his audience. The folders act as containers for notes jotted on a scrap of paper or quotes from an article he likes. When he's ready to write on that topic, he already has a wealth of content and thoughts to pull from!

It's a powerful practice to implement, especially if you plan on writing more than one book. If you've started this writing journey, be prepared for God to speak to you and inspire you for more writing projects.

Now that you're locating great content, here are some quick tips to help you take the kind of notes that will carry over into good writing.

NOTES ON TAKING NOTES

You're geared up. You have your pen and pad ready and you've downloaded a few productivity apps on your phone. Now let's look at expert ways to capture information that will support your writing.

Take brief notes with the main idea represented.
Phrases and keywords should jog your memory of what was important to you. Make sure you notate enough of the idea to trigger recall based on what you want to remember. The exception to this is what I term "power" quotes…

Take down "power" quotes word for word.
This is the exception to maintaining brevity in notetaking. Accurate quotes can distinguish a strong writing piece validated by an authority from a weak piece lacking credibility.

Take powerful statements down word for word to repurpose later and gain the reputation of someone who quotes accurately. Those who have worked with me know that I often take prolific notes—always listening for power quotes to use in upcoming writing.

With that in mind, you don't always need to include someone's entire thought in a quote, as long as you know how to format quotations properly. If you only pull the most powerful part of a quote, use an ellipsis to notate the break or signal that this is an excerpt from the original (...). If a word is missing or implied, use brackets to include the missing part where it is needed for clarification [brackets].

Learn to listen for clues about what's important.
If you're in a classroom setting, at a gathering, or listening to a podcast, be ready to write when someone says something like, "The main reason for this is..." or "There are four points to remember..." or "The heart behind this new book is...," etc. If you listen for these signals, you'll capture important information that others may miss.

Be organized in your notetaking.
Consider setting up a folder system to organize your notes and create a note-taking system that works for you. Use abbreviations that you will readily recognize. Consider indenting, adding bullet points or numbering notes. Use certain colors to categorize different topics. Develop a technique that will help you organize the train of thought. Have a plan in place to capture good content.

Review your notes for better retention!
I always review my notes after a meeting or Zoom call or event. I mark the page with my red pen, underlining or circling important points or quotes that impacted me or that I feel will be useful in future writing. Colored pens and highlighters can make it easy to identify the main points you want to pull out for your writing.

On some Zoom meetings or webinars, I have two pens in hand: red and black. I take notes with my black pen, while highlighting action points (my to-do list after the meeting) or important points in red. This system simplifies follow-up. What's most important is to develop a notetaking system that will help you get ahead of the curve for follow-up or notating the memorable moments.

I hope this chapter has been helpful to you. Follow through, and you'll always have good content, a new perspective, or even new vocabulary to incorporate into your writing.

One last story: I recently attended a high-level gathering of business and nonprofit leaders. As I took notes on the meeting's content, I also jotted down a few new words to add to my vocabulary! It was refreshing to be with people in a different circle of influence than my norm, and I went into the day of meetings as a learner. In the same way, I encourage you to be prepared, listen and observe for good content in new settings.

EXERCISES

1. Content is king for good writing! Think of a current writing project and list all the possible sources of great content. Include interviews, trade magazines, internet articles, books—anything that represents a good, reliable source specific to your topic.

2. Develop a plan and a system for taking notes in various settings. For example, I use an app called AudioMemos for recording messages on the go and interviews (with permission). The Notes section on my smartphone holds what I need to jot down quickly and my new favorite app is Captio which emails my note to my inbox. I carry a notebook or padfolio with a favorite pen for events or meetings.

Determine what will work best for you and write your organization plan here:

Finding great content and taking great notes is part of your writing arsenal! Before moving on, take a quick inventory of your toolbox. You've taken steps to kick obstacles out of the way and developed the disciplines of a writer—thinking like one, writing every day, reading, observing and growing!

You're armed with the four key development questions to help you write across various mediums on topics that will intentionally engage your hoped-for audience. You've gained insight on where to find great content, plus tips on ways you can always have something to write about. You'll never be stalled for content!

Now, let's look at how to structure good writing and develop a piece.

5

THE BEGINNING, THE END AND ALL THE PARTS IN THE MIDDLE

STRUCTURE AND ORGANIZATION

"You make known to me the path of life..."
Psalm 16:11 NIV

Have you ever been on a road trip with a friend and gotten lost? After hours of wrong turns and dead ends, the fun has seeped out of the adventure and you just want to get home... kind of like the time I went hiking in the woods with my granddaughter.

It was fun at first. The path wound in and out through the forest, over creeks and through ravines. We talked the whole way! Too quickly, the sun started setting and I realized I had no idea how to get out of the woods and back to our car. My concern grew as it became dark and the way out became more and more elusive. We made it out, but next time we'll take a map!

The idea of a free-spirited road trip sounds adventurous, but it can end in disaster. Unfortunately, that's how some writers operate.

Starting your writing project with a loose let's-see-where-this-leads mentality can be great for free-flowing writing or brainstorming. It can be helpful when you want to give your creativity room to breathe, to explore and dream and consider the possibilities—the rabbit trails that may prove insightful or the side jaunts that could open up new perspectives.

But after you've considered the possibilities, at some point you have to land on a structure. You have to decide what exactly you want to say and *how*. This is where you start working out exactly what this book, article or script will look like.

If you don't take the time to think your structure through and plot your course, you'll wander in the forest and never find your way out. You'll waste precious writing time and the fun will slowly fade as you fight your way out of the woods or the weeds to express what you want to say effectively. It gets worse if you've got a deadline looming close.

With your four key development questions thought through, it's time to organize your thoughts to achieve the most compelling piece. Let's look at the three basic parts of writing structure.

THREE PARTS OF STRUCTURE

Structure is important. You'll accomplish more—and be a faster writer—if you think of your writing in three parts: a beginning, middle and end. You might also think of these as the:

- Intro

- Body

- Conclusion

Imagine a cord running throughout your writing, an unbroken thread that connects the intro to the body to the conclusion. You maintain continuity in your writing by maintaining your stream of thought throughout. You should know where you're starting——where you're going—and the path you intend to take there!

Here's the exciting part: you've already done a lot of the heavy lifting by developing your work using the four key development questions. You know your what, your who, your medium, and your why.

In other words, you know where you're going (your goal or call to action). Now it's a matter of determining the best and most engaging road to get there as you flesh your piece out on paper: your path that joins the what to the why, the A to the B.

If you've lost your way, you've almost certainly lost your reader. <u>Don't break the cord.</u>

Outlining for Success

As you organize your thoughts, look for main headings and subheadings. What are the main points you want to share? What bits of information or thoughts support another thought or idea? Which ideas go together or work towards a certain slant that would interest your reader?

Pull those out and organize them into a "working outline." This is not the fancy I, II, III outline you did in high school, although you may need to develop an in-depth outline depending on the writing project.

Don't shy away from creating a formal outline to organize thoughts towards a more extensive project such as a book, or a script outline for your screenplay. However, for shorter pieces, an informal or "working" outline should suffice with the main points and supporting details or thoughts jotted down.

This simple organization will direct you as you write and help keep the dots connected from beginning to end. Plus, it will make it easy to spot areas in your piece that are weak or unsupported or just don't work to validate what you want to say. In those cases, your outline is your friend! In the early development phase, outlining can help you finalize your topic and what you want to say —or choose another topic or slant if necessary.

Let's look more closely at the three main parts of your writing piece which will lead to building a working or a formal outline.

THE INTRODUCTION (THE BEGINNING)

Depending on your medium, you may only have a few words or sentences (or minutes for a film) to capture the attention of your potential reader or audience. Lose them in the introduction, and you've lost your opportunity to speak into their lives.

Pique their interest in chapter one of your book or page one in your screenplay, and you're more assured to keep your reader engaged throughout the entire manuscript.

An easy example to look at for generating interest is the piece of promotional copy you write when your book launches and goes live on Amazon. What's more interesting in how this promotional copy opens? What's the best way to start this "journey" of a read:

John Doe's new book is great. It will help you find the perfect home for your family and help you remodel quickly...

OR

Ready to find that perfect home for your family? John Doe's latest book, "Move in Now!" will jumpstart your house-hunting and settle you into your new dream home quickly...

Can I be honest? A lazy writer will be quite happy with the first example. If it's John writing it, he may feel he's said what he wanted to say (his new book is great) and he hopes it's enough to tease the reader to read to the end and buy his new book. Plus, he's tired! He's just written the book and he's ready to move on.

A smart writer will take the time to write a compelling piece, no matter the writing style (and no matter how tired they are!). They will not assume that people will read their work. They understand that they've got to win the attention of today's reader who is assaulted with multiple messages everywhere they turn. Text messages, advertising, emails—the list of the distractions you've got to fight through as a writer to capture audience attention goes on and on.

I'm not advocating "shock" writing; I'm talking about taking the time to elevate your work and make it worth reading, beginning with a strong opening. And while you are doing that, keep the face of your intended reader in mind.

Capture Your Audience with Good Writing

A good writer (that's you) will take the time to use interest techniques to captivate your reader from the start. This is where discipline and the hard work of writing come in. You can't be lazy or naively assume that people want to read your thoughts.

Grab hold of your reader in your introduction and don't let them go. Avoid boring, avoid cliches, avoid making this all about you. Instead, think of your avatar, your target audience.

What will capture their attention? What are they thinking about? What are their pain points, their needs or wants or desires? What are they seeking solutions for? How can you reach them in those first sentences or first chapter and spark their interest?

As a writer, you must wisely consider how you will open the piece and then deliver on that promise. Which brings us to the main body of your writing...

THE BODY (THE MIDDLE)

The body of your work is where you support the topic of your writing. Examples, stories, statistics and other details help build the case for your main point—your "what do you want to say."

Remember the content gathering skills you added to your writing wheelhouse from the previous chapter?

Now you get to put those skills to strong use! Your content will inform your decisions in developing and building out your writing. And, as you structure your piece with a working outline, you'll be able to easily see where you have holes or missing pieces or simply need to do more research to write a great selection.

This is where an overheard conversation adds interest, a hard but revealing statistic brings the topic home, or a "power quote" or verse from the Bible validates what you want to say to your intended audience while leading them to your goal of writing.

The medium you're working in coupled with knowing your audience and what will interest them will help you make the right choices for building out the body of your work—the gist of what you want to communicate.

Let's look at a few techniques to help you add interest to your writing. As we do, think of your current writing project and consider what will best support your topic. Much of this applies to non-fiction writing, but even for fiction I think you'll find ideas that will help you with story building. Be open to ideas that will help you tell a good story well.

1. Give Examples

Appropriately chosen, examples strengthen your writing and add interest. Examples help ground your topic and make it easier for the reader to grasp. They move your thoughts from your head to the heart of your audience, helping them visualize what it is you're talking about.

For instance, if you're writing an article to encourage urban gardening among millennials, do your research and be prepared to give examples. General statements will not carry as much weight as a specific example.

If you want to say that urban gardening is a relaxing hobby, my next question would be, "How so?" Can you give me an example?

You might say something like this:

Urban gardening offers an escape from the stresses of life.

OR

After a hectic workday, harvesting kale from my urban garden relaxes my mind and helps me breathe again.

2. Tell a Story

Use stories—your own or someone else's—to make your point. Bring in the human perspective and you'll help others better relate to your writing.

Are you writing a blog about fitness or health? Maybe you've decided to tackle the subject of caffeine consumption and the value of cutting back. Pop in a personal story of your struggle to drive past Starbucks without stopping. A good story helps people relate.

Also, remember that humor is a great tool to incorporate into your writing in the proper context. If you're writing a book to help married couples weather the challenges of raising kids, blending families, or surviving a financial crisis, you may want to use humor to ease into the subject matter. A funny story can disarm the reader to receive what you have to say, especially on a sensitive issue.

3. Give Reasons, Benefits and Statistics

Compelling reasons or benefits can offer strong support for your main topic. For example, if you're writing a book about resolving race issues in our country, what reasons will support your proposed plan?

In the same way, if you're a pastor writing a blog to encourage people to attend a Sunday morning service, first you'll have to convince them to get out of bed on their day off. A compelling benefit will help. Are marriages getting stronger at your church? Are young adults more successful in their life and work because of the faith community? Do you serve doughnuts and coffee? What will help a person get out of bed and join you at church? Give a good reason or benefit.

Depending on the type of writing, statistics also add depth, meaning and validity to your writing. If you're covering the topic of PTSD and homelessness among war veterans to compel people to action, solid statistics give a reason to help that people can't deny. If your topic is strengthened with statistics, confirm your source as reliable and the stats as current.

Depending on your topic and audience, scriptures are also a powerful way to support your piece. God's word offers multiple reasons and benefits—on numerous life topics—for living the life God intended or showing the path from a problem to a solution.

4. Compare or Contrast

Another technique to support your work is comparing or contrasting two or more different things. What's different? What's similar? This can help people grasp the depth of what you're saying.

For example, this technique will help when writing a testimonial of what God has done in your life. General comments like "I feel amazing" or "I am a changed person" won't help the reader understand what's happened to make you feel that way.

If you compare yourself now with how you *used* to be, you've gained your reader's interest. If you were depressed before but now you've found great joy, that's a contrast people can appreciate. Using comparison and contrast is a great tool to increase your writing impact.

THE CONCLUSION (THE END)

The conclusion is the ending point where you tie your intro, body and closing thoughts together. This is also where you accomplish your goal or present your call to action, which will be easy to do if you've maintained a cord throughout your writing.

If you've written well, your reader will be right there with you, ready to take the next action step. Don't leave the reader hanging. If you've kept them this long, you owe it to them (and yourself) to answer the subconscious question, "What do I do now?"

In marketing web copy or social media posts, the call to action is often very obvious:

Sign up now!

Watch the video here.

In other types of writing, you'll employ more subtle ways to encourage the reader to move towards your goal. For example, if you've written an article stressing the importance of reducing caffeine consumption, you may offer steps to slowly cut back. Your well-written novel may accomplish your goal of instilling hope for broken relationships simply through the beautiful telling of a restored marriage.

A screenplay about an underdog who wins the day will have your audience cheering when the credits roll if you've done your work well. They'll walk out of that movie theater inspired to tackle their personal challenges with greater resolve.

The four key development questions from Chapter 3 will solidify your goal or call to action *before* you start writing. If you worked through those in the development phase, you've established a clear target to aim at that will inform every writing decision. This makes it easy to accomplish what you set out to do by the time you reach your conclusion or ending.

Throughout your writing, be cognizant of maintaining continuity—the integrity of your cord or stream of thought running through your introduction, body and conclusion. Construct an unbroken thread and you will preserve your reader's attention all the way to the end.

Choose a Technique

If you ever felt like you wanted to write "about" something, but didn't quite know how to go about it, congratulations. Chapter 3 armed you with the development process to help solidify what you want to say and why, and now you've added to your writing arsenal with techniques to flesh out your main topic towards your overall intention.

If you ever flounder, just come back to this list and consider: what technique will best support my topic? Which will be most engaging for my audience? A personal story? Hard-hitting statistics? Typically, you'll employ several strategies for your work to engage readers.

Remember all writing will have a beginning, a middle and an end. (This is your very basic outline.) Your development questions and decisions on telling your story or writing your nonfiction piece will lead you and your reader to a satisfying ending or conclusion.

You are well on your way to becoming a writer who can quickly come up with ideas and flesh them out in powerfully engaging ways. Test it out with these simple exercises.

EXERCISES

1. Think through the structure you would use on a topic of your choice. You may consider your current writing project or have a little fun choosing a sample topic. First, work through the four development questions.

1. What do I want to say?

2. Who do I want to say it to?

3. What medium am I writing for?

4. What is my goal or call to action?

2. Next, sketch out a simple outline. How will you introduce this topic? What techniques will best support it? How will you wrap this up in your conclusion? Consider examples, stories, reasons, benefits, statistics and comparison/contrast techniques. Jot your ideas here:

- **Topic:**

- **Introduction (beginning):**

- **Body (middle):**

- **Conclusion (ending):**

Thinking through structure and order will help you write intentionally and effectively. But wait—there's more! In our next chapter, we'll look at power writing skills. If you can master these, you'll have bumped up your writing skills yet another notch!

6

Power Writing Skills and Construction

Elevate Your Writing Quickly

"... my tongue is the pen of a skillful writer."
Psalm 45:1 NIV

Do you have a passion to write? If you've worked through each chapter and explored new ways to approach your writing, the dream of your novel, blog or completed screenplay is within reach!

You've moved the dial and you're closer than ever before to becoming a writer. Not just an ordinary writer, but one who can wield the pen (or the keyboard) adeptly, writing for your intended audience while capturing their attention and their hearts.

In this chapter, you'll gain the power writing skills to construct a strong first draft and guide the editing process. First, let's review what we covered in Chapter 5 about structure and organization.

When you get a great idea or are given a writing assignment, brainstorming the topic is a powerful way to start organizing your thoughts. What are all the possible options or slants you can take? Let yourself explore and discover before you land on what you really want to say about that topic, while keeping your target audience in mind.

Too often writers fall in love with a great idea before considering if it's relevant to who they're writing to or for. A skilled writer writes with their audience avatar in mind and then, takes the time to structure their work in a way that keeps the reader with them from beginning to end.

Your Outline Is Your Skeletal Structure

Structure is important. As you approach each writing project, keep in mind that all writing will have a beginning, middle and end: an intro, body and conclusion with a cord that runs through it, keeping your thoughts connected and your reader engaged.

As you organize your thoughts, remember that your outline is like the skeleton you will flesh out as you write. If you're working on a book or larger project, a formal outline will be exactly what you need to take you to the finish line. However, for shorter projects such as a blog or article, a simple working outline will guide you there.

We've covered a TON of ground and you're probably chomping at the bit to put it all into action. First let's arm you with power writing skills to make your first draft stronger and the editing process easier.

I often refer to these skills as "wordsmithing." Let's take a look...

8 POWER WRITING SKILLS

Even brief phrases and sentences can become powerful strokes of the pen when you've thought through word usage and construction. Before you tackle your first draft, you'll save yourself (and your editor) a lot of grief and time if you write with these skills in mind.

I've identified eight power writing skills. I'm sure there's more, but these are the ones I find most lacking when I'm asked to edit someone's work. Apply these to your writing and you'll stand out like a pro!

1. Write in the Positive

How often have you read something that begins with "not only" or "don't"? It's a fast way to weaken your writing and turn your audience away.

Start your writing with "don't" and you can quickly turn your reader off with your negative stance. People don't like to be told what NOT to do. Can you turn your "not only" and "don't" into something positive?

Years ago I was tagged to develop an online radio station. Branding, marketing and promotion were all on my plate, as well as acquiring the music and navigating the logistics of paying royalties. The station's uniqueness was the type of music we played: praise and worship music that brought hope and uplift to the listener.

It was tempting to say something like "not only will you hear great music..." or "you don't want to miss the music"—but my goal was to find a tagline that would brand the radio station in a positive light. The branding we finally landed on was:

"More than great music... it's LIFE!"

More often than not, your writing will be stronger and more clear if you write in the positive. For example:

"Not only were the prayers comforting, but..." could be revised to read **"The prayers were comforting and..."**

"Don't miss this event..." can be turned into **"Attend and experience..."** or **"Sign up now to experience..."**

"*Not just* great music" was brainstormed to become **"More than great music..."**

See the difference? Write positively. It will increase the impact of your words.

2. Use Strong Nouns and Verbs

It's easy to spot quickly written novels by novice authors, masters of the overuse of adjectives and adverbs. Romance novels seem to be most notorious for over-reliance on these modifiers.

The old woman walked slowly to the couch.

It works. We get it. But what if we were to take the time to paint a better visual with a stronger and more descriptive verb? The same sentence above could be revised to read:

The hag limped to the couch. (or staggered or slumped or struggled...)

Simply replacing the adverbial phrase "walked slowly" with a strong verb paints an entirely different picture! Taking it a step further, if we replace the adjectival phrase and noun with something more descriptive, we create an amazing visual. What about this...

The heiress staggered to the divan. (or the nurse or lawyer or suspect or spy... to the examining table or bench or davenport.)

What visual does this sentence paint now? Notice that our revised sentences are shorter and more succinct than the original, yet they present stronger images.

Effective writing relies upon descriptive, strong nouns and verbs and avoids overusing adverbs and adjectives. It takes more brain effort to come up with a strong noun or verb, but the pay-off is well worth it for a piece that uses word economy and is well-written.

Make every word count. Replace generalities and neutral words with strong and descriptive nouns and verbs. For example, why use the word "man" when you could use the word agent, soldier, father, or executive? Why say he "walked noisily up the stairs" when you could say he stomped or marched or "clattered up the stairs"?

One word of caution: sometimes the best word for a piece is the simple verb "walked" or "said." Find the balance in your writing.

3. Be Succinct

Avoid wordiness! Sometimes we add words simply because we can. We may free-flow in an attempt to express everything on our hearts; however, at some point we have to do the hard work it takes to express ourselves succinctly. As noted above, we painted a brilliant picture with fewer words, simply by putting some brainpower into the writing.

Without honing in on exactly what we want to say, that extra verbiage becomes an easy way to lose your reader, whether through boredom or confusion.

Good word economy begins with Power Skill #2 as you replace adjectival and adverbial phrases with more robust and descriptive nouns and verbs. You can take this further by recognizing extra words that add nothing to your piece.

Instead of saying, "The farmer bought a brand new pair of jeans," you could say he bought "a new pair of jeans." If something is brand new, it's new, right? And if it was critical to slash your word count even more, you could simply say "new jeans" instead of "a pair of new jeans."

This becomes a critical skill when your word count for a project is limited by space or requirement. If the guidelines for an article submission is a word count of 400, then every word counts! Imagine the squeeze when the submission requirement for a piece of writing is only 400 *characters* versus 400 words.

Eliminate unnecessary words. Your writing will be tighter and more impactful, with less chance of losing your reader.

A quick tip: if you're writing in Word, you can quickly check your word and character count by highlighting your work and then choosing "tools" in the menu above. It's a tool I often use in my writing.

4. Write in Threes

The eye and brain respond well to things in groups of three. Three candles set together appeal more than two. Three phrases connect the brain more than two. For example, you could express the thought below in several ways:

> The church is changing lives and encouraging families.

> The church is helping all ages connect to their destiny.

OR

The church is changing lives, encouraging families and helping all ages connect to their destiny!

Somehow the group of three completes the thought best in this instance. Of course, you never want to overwork this power skill, but it's nice to keep in mind.

5. Choose Verbs Wisely

Use the active voice versus the passive voice whenever possible and appropriate in your writing. For example:

"The screenwriter <u>typed</u> the words 'fade out'" is stronger than "The screenwriter <u>has typed</u> the words 'fade out.'"

"The student <u>finished</u> her term paper" is stronger than "The student <u>has finished</u> her term paper."

Also, use your brainpower to use descriptive verbs in lieu of the "to be" verb form when appropriate. For example, "Amy teaches well" is stronger than "Amy is a good teacher."

Think through your verb usage! Maintain consistency in verb tense and subject/verb agreement, but always watch for areas that could be made stronger or more concise with a more active tense or a different verb.

6. Use a Thesaurus

Whether you use a hardbound book or an online version, a thesaurus stretches your vocabulary and keeps your writing interesting. You never want to overwork a word, especially in a shorter body of writing.

Are you writing a press release about your new book? Don't overwork the word "new." Check a thesaurus and draw from other options such as: latest, original, first, introductory.

If you're stuck in your writing, a thesaurus can inspire your creativity. If I'm searching for the right thing to say or a new thought to build upon my writing, sometimes I'll open my online thesaurus and start typing in words as a search-and-explore tactic. A word or phrase may jog my memory or inspire a new thought to round out my writing or extend a concept.

Make a thesaurus part of your writing arsenal.

7. Employ Parallelism

Nouns should match nouns, verbs match verbs, etc., when you have a situation where thoughts logically run "parallel." For example:

Jane is an exemplary organizer, speaker and she manages well. (not parallel)

Jane is an exemplary organizer, speaker and manager. (parallel)

Here's another example:

A lover of the outdoors, Scott runs, hikes and he also likes to go out in a kayak every weekend.
(not parallel – and pretty wordy!)

A lover of the outdoors, Scott runs, hikes and kayaks every weekend.
(parallel)

8. Utilize Figurative Language

Similes, metaphors, hyperboles and personification can captivate your reader when used skillfully—and if appropriate to your genre. The Bible offers powerful examples of figurative language.

Similes are a form of comparison using the words "like" or "as." One thing is *like* another.

"He is **like a tree** planted by streams of water..." (Psalm 1:3)

Metaphors are an implied comparison. You are saying one thing *is* another.

"For the Lord God **is** a sun and shield..." (Psalm 84:11)

Hyperboles convey meaning by exaggeration. It's a "hyper" picture of something!

"They asked each other, '**Were not our hearts burning** within us while he talked with us on the road and opened the Scriptures to us?'" (Luke 24:32)

Personification is the art of giving human characteristics to inanimate objects.

"... all the **trees of the field will clap their hands**..." (Isaiah 55:17)

The caution here is to avoid overuse and worn-out clichés like "the wind whistled through the trees" or "as smooth as a baby's bottom."

Be intentional when you write and empower yourself with these eight skills. Employ them in your writing and you'll find that the better your writing becomes, the less editing required.

Let's turn our attention to "power construction" skills which add an extra punch to your writing. Want to be recognized as a professional? Apply these tips on sentence construction and continuity to your work. (You'll get to put all these to work in the exercises at the end of this chapter!)

POWER CONSTRUCTION

Attention to construction can distinguish between an average and a best-selling novel, a blasé or a well-read blog. Strive for the best and you will excel.

SENTENCE CONSTRUCTION
Choose what you want to stand out or emphasize.
The last words in a sentence carry the most weight. Take a look:

The pastor closed his Bible and sat down.

OR

Sitting down, the pastor closed his Bible.

What's most important? What do you want to emphasize? The sitting down or the closing of the Bible? If you want to emphasize the closing of the Bible, choose the second version.

Switch the word order in your sentences for variety.
Typical word ordering in a sentence is subject-verb-object. It's what we expect in writing. If you want to add interest to your writing, you can switch up the word order from time to time.

For example, take a look at this sentence:

> The book was written as a resource for
> gardeners to create urban gardens.

For variety, it could be written this way:

> Written as a resource for gardeners, the
> book helps them create urban gardens.

This switch-up in sentence construction can keep your reader on their toes and engaged. The one caution is to be intentional. Overwork this interest technique and your writing will appear forced, running the risk of driving the reader away.

CONTINUITY DEVICES
Use transitional words and phrases.
Remember the cord that runs through your writing, from beginning to middle to end? For larger bodies of work, use transitional words and phrases to keep the flow going from paragraph to paragraph. Words such as:

in other words, additionally, secondly, similarly, in conclusion, finally

These transitional devices pull your reader along through your writing and lead towards better coherence of thought.

Repeat key words and phrases.

Another continuity device for longer works employs the repetition of key words and phrases. Though you want to avoid redundancy, referring to a term you introduced earlier will maintain continuity, keeping you and your reader on topic.

For example, if you're developing an article about the friendliness of your congregation, you may mention that visitors feel at home quickly. Make a point of sprinkling the word "home" within your piece, and you will carry the reader along to finally want to come "home" to your church!

TO SUMMARIZE

I use power writing skills and intentional power construction every time I write. I only wish more writers would take the time to "wordsmith" their work before sending it to me for an editorial or script consultation! Don't be a lazy writer. Discipline yourself to wordsmith your work. It takes brainpower, but you can do this. I believe in you! Your writing can stand out.

EXERCISES

1. Stir your creative energy by writing at least three descriptive nouns to replace the general ones below. (For example, consider the general noun "baby." What other words could be used in place of baby? I thought of toddler, infant, bambino, newborn, etc.) Now it's your turn!

Glass:

Car:

Dog:

2. Can you think of three strong verbs to replace the adverbial phrases below? (For example, consider the verb-adverb phrase "drove quickly." We could use a single strong verb in place of that adverbial phrase, like: sped, raced, blazed.) Have fun brainstorming!

drove quickly:

Talked quickly:

Ran energetically:

3. Are you ready to do the hard work of wordsmithing your projects? Of the eight power writing skills, which one stood out most to you? Describe here.

Remember way back at the beginning of this journey when we talked about the disciplines of a writer?

    1. **Think like a writer.**

    2. **Read good writing.**

    3. **Discipline yourself to write daily.**

    4. **Ruthlessly edit your material.**

Guess what? Incorporating the power skills of this chapter into your work will enable you to carry out the fourth discipline to "ruthlessly edit your material." Your eye will notice weak nouns and verbs, unnecessary or redundant phrasing, and boring construction. You are well on your way to becoming a GREAT writer.

In the next chapter, I'll share my process for writing, plus a revision checklist and proofing guidelines to help you aim for excellence.

7

THE WRITING PROCESS AND REVISION GUIDELINES

HOW TO WRITE BETTER AND FASTER

"And whatever you do, whether in word or deed, do it all in the name of the Lord
Jesus, giving thanks to God the Father through him."
Colossians 3:17 NIV

It happens to the best of us. You've proofed and finally gone to print or posted on the internet—and then it happens. You get the email from a friend or the Facebook message: "Did you know you have a typo in your book?" You cringe inside, wondering what other errors you missed.

Finishing a first draft is a reason to celebrate. Don't let that moment pass you by! But after the first draft comes the editing and proofing and notes. The cliché is true: writing is rewriting.

The best writers understand it's all part of the process. Professional writers can take notes from an editor or producer and apply or at least consider them without being swayed from maintaining their voice and their intent in a piece of writing.

It requires vulnerability to re-examine your work with a red pen in hand. It takes even more of a baring of your soul to ask someone else to review or proof your work. And when your writing goes to a professional editor, it's like giving away a bit of your soul. But if your goal is to become the best writer you can be—if your heart is to represent Jesus to the world in an excellent and compelling way—it's necessary.

I've grown used to receiving notes as a screenwriter writing for a producer or when I'm writing on assignment for another ministry or organization. Even when submitting my manuscript to my publisher, I have to be prepared to consider their edits.

Over time you get used to it and recognize that their notes are not personal. It's always to make the writing better. You have to remember that *you* are not on trial. We can *always* get better at our writing, and a second set of eyes on our work can help elevate or more accurately express what we want to say.

My husband and kids are my silver bullet for many of my personal writing projects. I value their input and fortunately, they've been happy to take a moment to look over a devotional or blog before I post it, or an email campaign before I hit "send."

One thing I've learned when sending material out to a friend or family member is to let them know what kind of input you're hoping for. Do you need a full proof of the material or simply to know if the content makes sense to them? Are you wondering if the plotline engaged them? Did they get lost in the narrative at all? Before someone takes their time to read your material, it's helpful for them to know what kind of input you are seeking.

If you work with an editor, you'll encounter different types of edits. A line edit addresses your content, writing style and tone, whereas a copy edit is focused on proofing: checking your grammar, punctuation and spelling as well as looking for typos. If you employ an editor or your publisher supplies one, it's important to know what to expect.

You'll be ahead of the game if you learn how to be ruthless with your work before it goes out to someone else. Take your writing as far as you can and then seek out an editor or a good friend who can look at your writing objectively and with your audience in mind.

This chapter is all about helping you do just that. First, let's look at a simple process you can apply every time you write.

A SIMPLE WRITING PROCESS

Writing is not rocket science, but it does help to have a plan and a process to guide you from start to finish. Remember, development is key.

The four key development questions are the foundation of your writing process. They will prompt you to consider what you want to say in light of *who* you want to say it to, and then on to consider the particulars of the medium you are writing for, and your goal or call to action.

In the next chapter, we'll look at the various mediums and their idiosyncrasies that you need to know. However, bear in mind that the concepts you've gained from page one to here apply, no matter what medium.

Now, on to the process: 8 simple steps you can take with each writing project.

THE 8-STEP WRITING PROCESS

1. Consider a topic. What do you want to write *about*?

2. Ask the four development questions. Brainstorm as you consider the best way to develop the topic in light of your intended audience.

- What do I want to say?

- Who do I want to say it to?

- What medium am I writing for?

- What is my goal or call to action?

3. Structure your writing. Organize your thoughts into a working outline with a beginning, middle and end. (For more significant works such as a book, your outline will be more in-depth.)

4. Fill in any blanks with more research or information-gathering. If you've organized well, you should be able to spot the holes in your writing easily.

5. Write your first draft.

6. Print your work and ruthlessly edit! Make revisions and research further as necessary to fill in any further gaps in each new draft.

7. Proof your work.

8. Lock in your final draft and post or publish.

Again, your goal is to make the writing the best you can before asking a trusted person to review or proof your draft, or before it goes out to an editor for a line or copy edit. Now let's look more closely at the revision and proofing process.

REVISION GUIDELINES

You've finished your blog, web article, print magazine article or book, but your work is not yet completed. What you hold in your hand is a rough draft. For professional writers, it's time to work towards a polished final draft ready to be printed, uploaded or sent out.

These revision guidelines will polish your work to be the effective piece you hoped for. If possible, allow 24 hours to gain a fresh perspective before you revise your work, and longer for a larger body of work! Some authors like to set aside their novel for a month and then come back to it with fresh eyes.

Print a hard copy of your work and have a red pen in hand to circle areas that are weak or need revision. This is where you put all your newfound skills to work: power writing skills, power construction skills, and the structure savvy you've gained to capture your reader's interest at the beginning and keep them reading through to the end with an unbroken cord.

Review those earlier chapters and checklists as necessary before diving into your revisions. Then, work through the following ten-point revision checklist. This is where courage and honesty become a part of your writing arsenal. You'll need them to be able to edit your work ruthlessly.

We're aiming for excellence (not perfection): a piece that will engage readers and accomplish your goal to enlighten, encourage, inspire or entertain.

Ready with your red pen? As you work through the checklist, circle areas in your piece that need attention. Slash through words or phrases that weaken your work. Pretend it's someone else's work if need be! This is all part of the process.

10-POINT REVISION CHECKLIST

1. Are your main ideas supported by concrete details?

2. Are there any continuity breakdowns? Do you maintain your cord of thought throughout?

3. Are there any nouns or verbs that could be made stronger or more visual?

4. Do you see any unnecessary words or phrases? Places where you could use a strong noun or verb instead of an adverbial or adjectival phrase?

5. Are sentences varied in length and structure for interest?

6. Do you overuse any words?

7. Do you have an engaging opening sentence?

8. Is your concluding paragraph or sentence strong?

9. Have you said what you intended to say?

10. Have you accomplished what you intended to through this writing?

With your pages marked in red, now you're ready to go back and elevate your writing. Explore ways to make this piece better! Clear away confusion. Kick out boring. Eliminate the rabbit trails.

Make it more understandable, more interesting, more engaging for your reader! Hash through the problem areas until you are satisfied with your work. Empowered with your new-found writing skills, let your writing reflect your learning.

And, be encouraged. The more you write, the better you'll get. The more you're willing to be ruthless with yourself, the more impactful your writing will be.

Once you've made all those changes and you've gotten to your final draft, it's time to focus on proofing your work. Print the revised piece again, and with red pen in hand, do a final proof of your writing.

PROOFING FOR EXCELLENCE

Just as you did for revisions, print a hard copy of your writing project to proofread. Have a red pen in your hand to mark errors and do your best to look at this with a fresh perspective. If you have a friend or family member who is good at proofing and willing to help, they can be the "new eyes" that will catch the errors your eyes may miss.

Read slowly and do not skim. Reading your paper out loud can slow you down to catch inaccuracies and omissions. Some people work through their manuscript backwards to force themselves to examine each word, each sentence.

Proofread for:

1. **Misspelled words.** Do not rely on a spell checker for your final proof. It will miss the words that have varied spellings depending on usage.

2. **Typos.** These include extra words, spaces or lines between words or sentences.

3. **Punctuation errors.** When in doubt, use a grammar book to clarify proper punctuation.

Once you've proofed and corrected errors, print again and take one last look. Excellence does matter. Sloppiness in this area can reflect poorly on your work.

Although typos can get past us and end up in a blog that you just posted or a book that went to print, perform your due diligence in revising, editing and proofreading. Typos can have serious consequences, so allow time for this step in your writing and revision process timetable.

One final word on editing and revising your work. Remember that "done" is better than perfect. Posted, published or produced is better than an unfinished book or screenplay that you are continually reworking. At some point, you have to write "The End." You have to type "Fade Out."

Don't allow yourself to be trapped into feeling that something is never good enough. The world is waiting for your voice, your words of light. And, they're waiting for the *next* blog or book you will write. Writing is rewriting—but sometimes you have to call it done.

EXERCISES

1. Print your most recent project and see if you can elevate it! Apply the power writing skills to make the piece more interesting and engaging. (Note: If you realize that the piece was never fully developed to be the best it can be, then go back to the four key development questions and start your revisions there.)

2. Proof your work! Look for misspelled words, typos and punctuation errors.

3. If you have a friend who's willing, ask them to take another look at your piece. Ask them if any areas were hard to understand. See if they recognize any weak spots. Find out if your goal or call to action was accomplished with them. And then...

4. With the notes from a trusted friend, take another pass at your work. Can you elevate it just a little bit more? Try it!

If you apply these revision and proofing guidelines to your work, I can guarantee your writing will improve drastically.

If you're working on a larger project such as a book or novel, include the hard work of revisions and proofing in your timetable. I know many professional writers who will do MULTIPLE passes on a project before they send it out to an editor or publish it. Don't be afraid of the revision process. This is part of the "think like a writer" discipline that is helping you become a professional writer.

You're in the home stretch now! Coming up next, we'll delve into the various mediums and how to approach writing in the digital age.

8

WRITING FOR DIFFERENT MEDIUMS—PRINT AND DIGITAL

UNDERSTAND THE NUANCES

"I have become all things to all people so that by all possible means
I might save some."
2 Corinthians 9:22 NIV

Want to be a faster writer? Follow the process. If you apply everything you've learned to this point, you will be able to write your first draft better and more quickly than you ever dreamed possible.

Take the time to develop your writing. When you get a great idea for a book or blog (or receive a writing assignment from a publisher or producer):

- Brainstorm the possible approaches

- Ask yourself the four key development questions

- Determine best structure (your beginning, middle, end)

- Apply power-writing and construction skills

- Write your first draft

- Edit ruthlessly

Rewrite as needed until you have an amazing final draft that's proofed and ready to go to print or post online!

Recently a fellow screenwriter sent his script to me, asking for input. He was an accomplished writer and had gained some success in Hollywood. Unfortunately, in reading his script, one thing stood out to me. The writing was subpar for someone of his caliber.

At some point in his career, he had stopped growing. Point blank, he assumed he had "arrived" and quit honing his craft.

Dear writer, don't let that be you. Never stop growing and learning. We can always get better. We have never arrived! I would cringe to go back and read my first article or screenplay. I'm sure I felt they were great at the time, but since then I've grown and changed. Hopefully my writing reflects that.

Always work to elevate your writing. You've made a conscious decision to do that and I applaud you. Keep going!

WHAT MEDIUM ARE YOU WRITING FOR?

With all your new and updated writing skills in hand, let's turn our attention to medium. Remember, it's essential in your development phase to know where your work will live, the medium you are writing for.

That's why it's key to ask yourself (or remind yourself) at the start: "What medium am I writing for?" Very simply, we can boil media down to two general categories: print and digital. Within those two groupings there are multiple variations, all with nuances that a good writer (that's you) gains adeptness and ability to meet.

Print media includes books (fiction and non-fiction), magazines, direct mail letters, processes, one-sheets, resumes, promotional cards, brochures, etc. And, at the outset, a script is written to be read before a producer decides to finance and greenlight it for production.

Digital media includes blogs, web articles, web content, eBooks, downloadable white papers, email campaigns, social media, online ads, etc.

Did you know that the writers of the Bible developed their writing similarly to what you're doing now? They were very conscious of what they wanted to say, who their audience was, their medium and their goal or call to action.

For example, read the book of Matthew and you'll realize he was writing toward a Jewish audience. What did he want to say? Jesus was the Messiah, fulfilling Bible prophecy. Matthew's goal was to convince his audience of the Lordship of Jesus Christ and motivate them toward fulfilling Jesus' final recorded words on earth: go forth and make disciples of all nations! (Matthew 28:19)

John's gospel was written towards Christian believers. What did he want to say? It's summed up in John 1:4 after he clearly stated that Jesus is the Word made flesh: "In him was life and that life was the light of all mankind."

John's goal or "call to action" rings clear in the final chapter of John 20. "Jesus performed many other signs in the presence of his disciples, which are not recorded in this book. These are written that you may believe that Jesus is the Messiah, the Son of God, and that by believing you may have life in his name." In other words, believe the scriptures; believe in who Jesus is!

The New Testament authors of the Bible have one thing in common: they were all writing for the print medium. (And, to be clear, they were all inspired by God to pen the words we hold dear as the Bible.) Their letters were shared from church to church and the gospel spread rapidly throughout the known world, partly because of the roads built by the Romans.

The Digital Age—A New Pathway for Glory

Today, the digital age has opened up a new pathway to reach the world. The internet offers multiple new ways to share the gospel and cover the earth with God's glory.

With every new opportunity comes a learning curve. As writers, extra work and study is required to enter the doors that are open before us in the digital age.

In other words, you can't (typically) take your written-for-print magazine article and copy and paste it into your website and expect success. At the very least, you'll keyword your title to gain better traction and discovery in the search engines. More shaping will be required to engage and maintain your online reader.

Readers scan when they're on their computers or their phones. That's why it's important to add links, shorten paragraphs and break up blocks of copy with headers and images. These stylizations help keep your online audience engaged.

However, before we dive too deeply into the digital medium, let's back up and talk about your print book or magazine article: your hardbound print material that readers will curl up with on a couch or study at a desk.

WRITING FOR PRINT

It's hard to completely disengage from digital media. Ultimately, your print book should live online as an eBook or audiobook as well as in hardcover form. And if you're writing a short story or article, many magazines publish both a hard copy and an online digital version of their publication. But you've got to get your book or article written first, so let's look more closely at how you develop your work for the print medium before exploring digital options.

If you're writing for print, everything we've discussed to this point applies. Development is key, and you'll follow the writing process to a T. But first, let's go way back to Chapter 3 and relook at the four keys to becoming a great writer:

1. Think like a writer.
2. Read good writing.
3. Discipline yourself to write daily.
4. Ruthlessly edit your material.

Let's especially look at number two: Read good writing.

Is there a book in your heart that you've been dreaming of writing? A magazine that you'd love to be featured in? Before you start writing, read. And as you read, you'll begin to find your voice, your USP or "unique selling point."

Consider authors like Charles Dickens, A.A. Milne, Jane Austin, J.K. Rowlings, David Baldacci, Frank Peretti, Max Lucado. These authors stand out because of their unique voice, style and tone.

Even magazines present a particular tone and style. *Magnolia* reads differently than *Shape* or *National Geographic* or *Birds & Blooms*. Most magazines or outlets have style guides for regular contributors, but you can grasp their style and how they shape content towards their particular audience simply by reading what they carry.

Read the material that will help you develop your voice, while exploring the different styles and tones appropriate for the particular print medium. Use your daily writing time to practice and discover your style.

Develop Your Voice

Want to become a writer that readers love to read? Your daily discipline of writing is your practice ground! Practice writing. Discover your unique voice, your unique way of sharing thoughts and ideas with others.

What resonates with audiences? What feels right and good to you? What fits the particular medium you are writing towards? Listen closely to the Holy Spirit of God as you become a writer that astounds others with a unique voice that shares depth or humor or insight.

Know the Genre

Genre refers to a class or category of your artistic endeavor that has a particular form, content, technique or style. Easy examples of fiction genres include thrillers, sci-fi and drama. A biography, testimony or devotional book could be classified as another category of writing. It's important to understand the genre as well as current trends so you can meet the genre expectations of your audience when you write.

Genre will determine tone, style and even word choices. A thriller reads differently than historical fiction. A romance novel reads differently than a book on building a garden shed.

For example, I was writing a blog recently and I had used the word "ignited" in a sentence. It really didn't fit the tone of what was intended to be an inspirational piece; it felt too explosive of a word for what I wanted to say in this particular genre. Now, if I had been writing a thriller, it may have been perfect!

Do you know what word I finally landed on? Sparked. So very close in meaning, but it carries a different connotation that was more appropriate.

Understand Audience Expectations for Your Genre

Learn what audiences expect from your chosen genre. For example, romance writers know that audiences will be disappointed if a "first kiss" doesn't happen before you type "the end." Action writers understand that readers will expect action set pieces that escalate throughout the novel or film.

One of the best ways to understand genres and audience expectation is to read the favorites. If you intend to write a Christian thriller, you may read secular thriller artists, but I would expect that you would also read Ted Dekker or Frank Peretti to see how they weave faith into their story for Christian thrillers.

If you love a good romance, read Janette Oke's *When Calls the Heart* series or watch the popular television series based on the book. Go on a mission to find out what audiences love about the genre you plan to explore in your writing.

It's great if you can embrace one genre and become known for that (i.e., Max Lucado and his devotional writings or Brock and Bodie Thoene for their historical fiction). However, it's beneficial to gain the skills to become adept in various styles.

A friend who writes technical manuals and processes shared with me her desire to expand her skills to creative writing. She's now on a journey of discovery as she learns how to express herself in a different way.

What genre do you aspire to? Learn the audience expectations and techniques for skillfulness in that genre. Now, let's talk more about the print medium and the book you may want to write and publish.

DEVELOPING YOUR PRINT BOOK

If your book project seems daunting, take a deep breath and realize that everything you've learned to this point applies! You already have the tools to develop your book manuscript.

You've done your research, reading *and* writing to express your unique voice and style. A larger project such as a non-fiction book or novel will require a more in-depth outline, but you'll still walk through the four development questions.

Your research on current trends will come into play as you develop and determine the outline for your print manuscript. For example, for a novice author, a novella of 70,000 words may be a better place to start than a 125,000-word novel. Although Dicken's *Tale of Two Cities* may be your favorite book, you'll have a hard time capturing an audience if you style your first book after this classic. Adjust accordingly so that you have optimal opportunity to publish and gain readership, especially for your first project.

If it seems like I'm oversimplifying the writing process for your book, I'll encourage you with something I heard recently from award-winning screenwriter Micky Fisher. Known for sci-fi films and TV like *Mars*, *Extant* (executive produced by Steven Spielberg) and *Reverie*, he boils the huge storytelling process of a movie or television series down to one initial question: "What is it you want to say by telling a story in this genre?"

Does that sound familiar? What do you want to say? Micky adds, "A cool idea is just a cool idea."

In other words, as we discussed way back in Chapter 4, your idea to write a book "about" prayer or gardening or about your testimony is just a "cool idea" until you hash out the four development questions and discover what you want to say in the genre.

So whip out a pad of paper and start brainstorming your book! Think about all the possibilities, and then narrow your topic down to what you want to say and to whom. Imagine your audience avatar—their needs, wants, desires; their problems and the solutions they're seeking or simply their desire for a good story or an intriguing narrative.

Form an outline that will carry your reader from point A to point B. Imagine the cord that runs through your non-fiction piece.

For this larger writing project, take the time to build out your outline with main headings, subheadings, and details to support your topic. Note where you have gaps and do more research and brainstorming to outline a work that will keep your reader with you and engaged throughout. You've got the skills and the know-how! (If you need a refresher, go back to Chapter 5 on structure and organization.)

Too often, writers open their laptops and just start writing. They've got the initial seed idea and they're excited to get it on the page! I get it, but I'll warn you that if you don't take the time to map this out with a solid outline, you will probably run out of steam around page 40—and then the book goes into a drawer until the unction strikes again. It could be months or years before you tackle writing again. All the while, someone is waiting for your words... and quite possibly, God is waiting for you to follow through because he's got a second book in mind for you to write—if you will only buckle down and finish the first!

An outline is hard work. But it will be your roadmap to success for your book or another large writing project like a screenplay or a novel. Get the outline done and the writing will seem like a breeze!

Follow the writing process we've covered in previous chapters. This is in your wheelhouse; set aside the time and the place for writing. Think like a writer and get this book finished.

A Word on Writing Fiction

Without spinning this book into a creative writing course, I want to reassure you that even with a fictional book, the four development questions will help you set the tone and carry your story through to a satisfying end. Your cord that ties all this together is the narrative arc of the story.

When developing a novel or fictional piece, you'll consider the story concept and then develop each character to tell the story while exploring the character arcs. You'll outline your A story, B story and possibly a C story or runner that moves the reader through the narrative. You'll consider what needs to happen in each chapter and make sure your "story engine" is strong enough for this novel or series that you've been dreaming about.

But before you go too deep into your story world and while you are in the early development phase, think through the question: What do you want to say? You may have an intriguing story with interesting characters and fantastic plot twists, but even with fiction, you'll have a theme, something you want to say with this book. Perhaps you want to say that love conquers all, that good triumphs over evil, or that God gives people second chances. Determine what you want to say through this narrative.

Then, who do you want to say it to? Is this young adult fiction? For kids? For adult readers? Gear your creative writing towards your audience.

What medium are you writing for? We've established this is for print, which gives you great freedom to write without some of the constraints of digital media.

Finally, what is your goal or call to action? Maybe you want to make people laugh or smile. Maybe you want them to close the book with a satisfying nod to acknowledge that, yes, life is like that! Perhaps you want to raise awareness for sex trafficking or PTSD and even though this is a fictional story with fictional characters, your goal is to move people to action or empathy.

Do you see how the development questions apply even when writing fiction? Trust me in this and take the time to develop your book, whether it is fiction or non-fiction.

Publishing Your Book

A final word on going to print with a larger project such as a book: if you have an agent or publisher, they'll help you walk through the writing and editing process of your book. Your success is their success and you can expect their help in the publishing process as you move towards your release date.

One caution to keep in mind is that the days of a publisher carrying the full weight of advertising and promotions are gone. Even with a publishing house, plan on self-promoting and doing all you can to create the buzz surrounding your book for its success.

I highly suggest David Baldacci's Masterclass for an inside view of the publishing process and working with an editor. Visit my writing resource page on my website for a quick link to subscribe to Masterclass.

If you are self-publishing, there is a wealth of material online and in print that will help you towards a successful book launch. If you're serious about a writing career, I highly suggest investigating SelfPublishing.com. Even if you're with a publishing company, you'll be inspired by their notes on promoting your book. (You can find them in my writing resources on my website.)

As I've mentioned before, a blog may be a better place for you to start, before you do the heavy lifting of a book project. It's an excellent way to find your voice and your audience. Plus, it offers an opportunity to evaluate and adjust as you keep an eye on the statistics available online to see what engages your readers. And, whether you self-publish or get picked up by a publisher, having a built-in audience before going to print with a book lends towards better success (and mitigates risk for the publisher).

Now let's delve more deeply into the various nuances you'll find in writing for the web.

WRITING FOR THE DIGITAL AGE

In case you didn't know it, we are in a digital revolution. The pandemic of 2020 (and beyond) thrust us into the digital age at an accelerated speed. If you weren't online, you are now. Even churches that may not have had an online presence were forced to develop a digital outreach to stay afloat during the shutdowns prompted by the recent pandemic.

Although it's presented its challenges, the digital age offers tremendous opportunities! Writing for the web is an entirely different animal than writing for print. Throw out your high school teacher's admonitions for writing class papers and grab hold of a new style that can literally reach someone across the world.

Optimize Your Content and Reach Your Online Audience

Keyword-rich writing, otherwise known as Content Optimization and Search Engine Optimization (SEO), represents web writing skills that are a science in themselves. Some people devote whole careers to the science of SEO! If you are writing primarily for the web, it will benefit you greatly to acquire at least a basic knowledge and understanding of these ever-evolving skills to optimize your web pieces.

For our purposes and because online optimization is continually evolving, we'll focus on the general guidelines for effective web writing in which you can incorporate simple but powerful keyword research and SEO skills.

Be Found

The bottom line when writing for digital media is that you want to be found by the search engines. People google everything! They're asking questions online and you want to be the one answering those questions or providing the solution. In a very simple manner, it boils down to including search terms—keywords that your audience avatar is googling—in your title and content, whether it's a blog, book or article.

Years ago, when the internet was just taking off and keywording became a critical component to web writing, I gathered focus groups to brainstorm keywords that our intended audience was searching for.

Now, there are apps that will help you discover the current trends, but you still have to put yourself in your audience's shoes. You have to think like they think, which is why it's so very important to ask yourself the four development questions as you determine "What do I want to say?" and *"Who* do I want to say it to?"

What Is Your Audience Searching For?

Imagine your ideal audience. What questions are they asking? What information are they searching for? What are the things they will ask Google that they're too shy or scared to ask a friend?

Just to be clear, I'm not talking about shoehorning a keyword into your blog simply because it's trending. Nor am I referring to the keyword-crammed articles that some people write merely to be "found" on the internet.

What I'm advocating is the organic inclusion of keywords into your title and content. The new term for this is Content Optimization. It begins with knowing your audience, researching keywords and phrases that they are searching for that applies to what you want to say, and then consciously and wisely integrating those keywords and phrases into your writing.

Conduct Keyword Research

Keyword research can inspire you in the development process and even in the brainstorming process. If you intend to write a book about God for GenZ kids, keywording the topic can help you slant your "what do I want to say" to the questions that GenZs are asking online.

Bear in mind that you can type a word in Google and it will pull up suggestions of what other people are searching for, however, these results can be skewed towards your past searches and preferences. I would not rely on that process for your keyword research.

A simple tool I like to use is KeywordsEverywhere.com . A free version can get you started, but the paid version offers monthly search volume, cost per click (CPC), and competition data.

Here's a very simple process for conducting keyword research:

1. Consider what your target audience is searching for online: your reader's questions or the information they're seeking.

2. Type related words into a search tool such as KeywordsEverywhere.com and see what pulls up.

3. Evaluate the search results:

- **Monthly search volume:** typically it's best to choose keywords with 1,000/month or more search volume.

- **CPC:** Cost per click gives insight into what it would cost to use this search term in an ad, each time someone clicks on it and over to your online content (i.e., your blog or website). If you're not planning on paying for Google Ads to promote your content, you can disregard this at the moment.

- **Competition:** Pay attention to this. If the competition for your keyword is high, you'll have a hard time showing up on the first page of your avatar's search!

Your goal is to discover keywords with good search volume and low competition. Ultimately, you'd like to be on the first page of someone's online search. That's a tough thing to do, but the more you learn the concepts of content and search engine optimization, the better your blog or article will be found.

As I mentioned, optimizing your content for the search engines is an entire science that is continually evolving. What works today can be outdated tomorrow as algorithms change. But simply understanding the value of including a well-performing keyword in your title and content will help your content be found online.

The better you get at this, the more your work will be discovered—and that's how your readership can grow. Write well, write smartly and you can gain a worldwide reach.

If you are writing for the web, take the time to learn and grow in this area. Here are the apps I recommend. They each have free versions or trials and educational material that will help you grasp the concepts of online content optimization.

Keywordseverywhere.com – This is a browser add-on for keyword research, offering monthly search volume, CPC and competition data.

AnswerthePublic.com – They offer further insights into useful phrases and questions people ask around your keyword.

Trends.Google.com – Explore what's trending simply and quickly on Google Trends. This can help you understand the context around the thoughts, feelings and behaviors of your audience.

VidIQ.com – This is extremely robust and takes you on a deep dive, particularly if you are on YouTube and writing descriptions for your videos.

If this feels way over your head, just bear in mind it's all about knowing and reaching your audience. God will guide you in this if you take the time to do a little extra learning on the topic of optimization.

Armed with a little bit of knowledge, your blog or book will find "your people" online. Now let's talk about the different styles of writing that you will employ for digital mediums.

WRITING STYLES FOR THE DIGITAL MEDIUM

You cannot typically take a great print article, post it on the web and assume you'll have good readership. Writing for the web is more brief and to-the-point than print. People scan when they're on the web and your work should accommodate for that.

Also, the big words you used to impress your high school teacher will not fly on the web. If your article or web content looks like work to read, people will pass by. You've got to make the transfer from using left-brain words to right-brain words when writing for the web.

Left-brain words are the words that encourage deep thinking. They're the words a professor uses to raise your intellectual level a notch. Right-brain words are easy to grasp and therefore make your writing easy to scan for information on the web. They appeal more to the emotional than the intellectual part of your brain, thus making them a better choice for strong calls to action online.

Here's a sampling of left-brain and right-brain words. Notice the difference between the right-brain words which are easy to read and the left-brain ones which force you to kick your brain into gear and think:

<u>**Left-Brain — Right-Brain**</u>

Difficult — Hard

Superior — Better

Utilize — Use

Request — Ask

Learn — Find out

Instruction — How-to

Donate — Give

Purchase — Buy

Receive — Get

Right brain words can gather an audience to you, as your writing will look easier to scan. Remember that most successful blogs are written at a 5th-grade level.

Web writing encompasses a variety of styles, although the concepts for web articles, copy, content and blogs are the same. The following are tried and true guidelines that typically work across the various types of online content. One note of caution: the internet and especially social media are ever-evolving platforms. Stay on top of current trends and adjust your style as necessary.

GUIDELINES FOR DIGITAL WRITING

Keep it Short and Sweet

Articles and blogs on the web are typically kept to 400-750 words. The exception would be a white paper, which allows for greater length. The rules continually fluctuate, so find what resonates with your reader.

Also, bear in mind that some topics can handle larger word counts and some outlets have readers that expect and look forward to longer pieces. This is where you must do the research for what's current, trending and appropriate for where this article or blog may live online.

Break Your Copy into Shorter Paragraphs
It's rare to find a web article with paragraphs longer than two sentences. You may even find the occasional one-sentence "paragraph." Be aware that people scan on the web and you'll cut your content and your paragraphs down in size.

Use Right-Brain Words
As detailed above, the best rule of thumb is to write for the emotional side of the brain instead of the intellectual for powerful web writing. The exception would be a website that naturally relies on technical terms to reach its intended audience of doctors, technicians, scientists, etc.

Use right-brain words for the tabs on your website and for calls to action. For example, people will be more inclined to click on "give" than they will "donate."

Optimize Your Article or Blog Titles
Titles should offer information to your reader and help with search results. Title your articles with keywords that will alert search engines that the content is about financial freedom or an inspirational true story or urban gardening. Add interest to your titles, but not at the expense of sacrificing search engine optimization.

Optimize Your URLs
Most web content management systems will allow you to customize a specific URL (web address) for your article. If you've chosen a good title based on your audience and well-performing keywords, the system's automatic URL should work well. However, be prepared to customize as necessary to include good, descriptive keywords.

Imagine parents searching online for something fun for their kids to do this summer. For example, the URL happydaycare.com/**summer-fun-for-kids** will show up better in search results than happydaycare.com/**rest-assured-this-su mmer** even though you may think it's a catchy title. Although parents want to "rest assured," they're probably not searching for that online (but quick keyword research can confirm that).

As long as the URL is not misleading as to the content of the article, blog or webpage, you can optimize these for better SEO.

Make Your Call-to-Action Count

Remember the fourth development question? What is your goal or call to action? A well-thought-out call to action will engage online readers further with your content. Correlate your call to action to the theme of the online piece.

For example, if you're writing a blog about your new book, link to a page to "find out more here" or "shop now!"

Perhaps you've written an article with testimonies of people recently healed during your church service. Give them a chance to visit or call in so they have an opportunity to be healed.

Your blog may close with a line like, "Need healing? Visit ABC Church today." Hyperlink your word "visit" to link to the webpage with the address and directions to the church and you're set.

Your call to action is a way to facilitate a deeper and continuing connection with your reader.

Organize in an Inverted Pyramid for Skimming

Online, people are skimming for information, so reliance on the Associated Press format of an inverted pyramid (like an upside-down triangle) for web copy will increase readership. Think of a standard news article that starts with the most important and time-sensitive information first, trickling down to items of lesser importance.

This inverted pyramid style works great for online readers who scan—and *then* decide if they want to know more by clicking on a link. If you bury the details of a special service or concert at your church on the web, people may give up reading before they get to your main intent or call to action.

Stylize Your Text for Easier Online Reading

Break up your copy with bullets and headings that entice the reader to keep reading. Bold the important details of the text and at times insert ALL CAPS to draw attention. (Bear in mind, however, that caps can distract if overused—or offend if the reader feels like you are YELLING at them! Get my point? Use sparingly.)

Add Links Within Your Copy

Hyperlinks within your copy can further engage the reader as they link to more information. The general rule of thumb is no more than one hyperlink per 100 words, and you must use caution if the link takes people off your website.

The benefit in linking to another website is the strength it affords in search engine optimization. The caution is that every time you link to another website, you lessen the chances of the reader following through on your main goal—the call to action. Therefore, make a wise determination before you possibly distract the reader away from your website. (Note: there is an SEO strategy of a "resource pillar page" that links to a variety of resources on other websites; for most content, you want to keep people on your website.)

Include Photos and Videos for Greater Engagement

Images increase audience engagement dramatically online! People love photos, memes and videos. If chosen strategically, they engage the reader far beyond the same article with no images.

CONCLUSION

To sum up, here are ten tips for online writing that will engage your online readers, bearing in mind that you must keep up with current trends in this everchanging landscape:

10 TIPS FOR ONLINE WRITING

1. Keep it brief: shorter pieces and shorter paragraphs.

2. Use right-brain words for increased readership.

3. Conduct keyword research and write key-word rich content to be discovered by search engines.

4. Optimize your titles and content with your researched keywords.

5. Customize the URL to include keywords.

6. Incorporate a strong and relative call to action.

7. Structure your writing in the inverted-pyramid form for skimming.

8. Use bolds, bullets, headers and caps to maintain reader interest.

9. Add hyperlinks where appropriate.

10. Include images and videos to engage the reader.

We've covered a lot of ground in this chapter! Just remember that no matter what medium you choose, the four development questions still apply.

They are your trusted "secret weapons" for writing effectively. The more you wield them, the better you'll get with each writing project.

Do you need a moment to breathe? Take some time to research the various resources I've offered in this chapter.

EXERCISES

1. Visit my website to see the writing resources I recommend at LauraWoodwor th.com/writing-resources. They can help you in your writing journey and career.

2. Research your genre! Find out what the audience expectations are so that you can meet those in your writing.

3. Explore the science of keyword research, content optimization and SEO. Look at what my recommended apps mentioned above offer. Also, take time to google and discover what's current in this ever-evolving realm online.

4. Use my "10 Tips for Web Writing" to revise current web content or create something new! Consider a topic of your choice, brainstorm and develop it with the four development questions, and then write a blog or online article bringing all your skills to the table!

We're getting near the finish line! Before we cross it, in the next chapter we'll explore some specifics concerning blogs and social media.

For many of you, writing a blog is a solid way to launch your writing career and cultivate an audience. Your online presence will be enhanced with a strong social media presence. Come with me as we look at current best practices in this—you guessed it—ever-evolving realm.

9

BUILD YOUR ONLINE PRESENCE—BLOGS AND SOCIAL MEDIA

ESTABLISH YOURSELF AS AN AUTHOR

"And whatever you do or say, do it as a representative of the Lord Jesus, giving thanks through him to God the Father."
Colossians 3:17 NLT

Have you started writing your dream project yet—that book or blog or article that's burning in your soul? If you have, then congratulations! You're on your way to impacting lives with your unique thoughts and perspective. I pray you bring God's worldview into your writing; the world needs hope and truth and life. It's in your hands as a Christ-follower.

If you haven't made progress, then I encourage you to take a long hard look at what's stopping you. What's holding you back? Has it been hard to fit it into an already busy (or overwhelming) schedule? Are you fighting the imposter syndrome? You can move past this! You can carve out 15 minutes or half an hour to write. God has given you a unique voice and somebody needs to hear what you have to say.

If you're still struggling with where to even start, relax. Go back to the four development questions and build from there.

Sketch out a working outline that supports what you want to say and takes you through to your call to action. It may be very simple and barebones, but this thought process will springboard your thoughts as you start putting flesh on it: supporting ideas under your main headings, then details to back it all up. Pretty soon you'll have a solid outline to write from and you'll be on your way to completing that dreamed-of project.

Writing for the Digital Age

You never know whose life will be impacted by your writing, especially in the digital age! Years ago, one of my assignments was to write a web article highlighting the marvelous testimonies of what God had done over the weekend at my church. Every Monday, I would review my notes and choose several of the best stories to capsulize for my 450-600 word article.

One weekend, a young mother shared a testimony about her special needs child. God had done something unique in his life during the weekend services, and she noticed a marked—and miraculous—improvement in his ability to relate socially with others. It was a testimony that brought tears to many eyes as she shared the years of struggle and her new-found hope as she witnessed God's intervention in her son's life.

I did my keyword research and wrote the article, optimizing my title and content with keywords that would identify the testimony online. Not long after, another woman visited the church with her special needs child.

She found the article online and her faith was stirred. Wonderfully, God did a mighty work in her child's life that weekend—and it all began with taking the time to optimize my content <u>so that it would be found.</u>

That's the power of the digital age. That's just one single story of a changed life simply because I optimized my online article, reaching a hurting mom halfway across the country.

You don't always know who your writing reaches or how many lives are encouraged through your article, blog, or book, but sometimes you do. Those moments are golden in the life of a writer.

YOUR ONLINE PRESENCE AS AN AUTHOR

Whether your goal is to write for print or digital media, you can't escape the digital age and the need to establish yourself online. It may be as simple as your author page on Amazon, but one way or another, you've got to have a presence on the web. You, the writer and author, have got to be found.

Blogs and social media are powerful ways to build your online presence. Ultimately, a website will help you cultivate relationships with fans and followers you gain on social media—or meet at your book signing!

Without getting too deep in the weeds of building a website and incorporating an email marketing strategy, let me briefly explain why a website is important to consider at some point in your writing career. Social media communication is inconsistent. It varies because of the ever-changing algorithms on Facebook or Instagram. However, you can gather names and email addresses on a website and establish consistent communication with your readers via email campaigns.

You'll find a wealth of information online to guide you through building a website, starting a blog, and carrying out the best current practices on social media. It would be fruitless for me to delve into those details now, because literally, algorithms can change overnight. What I tell you today will be outdated tomorrow.

What I do want to share with you are the foundational concepts of developing your blog and establishing yourself on social media platforms. Let's look at three key concepts that I often share with clients when I'm advising them on building their online presence.

3 KEY CONCEPTS FOR YOUR ONLINE PLATFORMS

Whether you are setting up a blog or creating your accounts on social media, there are three main elements to determine in the development stage (and then later in the writing stage):

1. Voice

2. Content

3. Consistency

Nail these three and you'll be well on your way to building a strong online presence that will, over time, gather fans and followers who love your unique take on life and enjoy reading what you have to say.

VOICE

What is your voice as you speak through a blog or a social media post? Who are you—and <u>what do you want to say</u> to the world? What is your overarching theme or message?

Are you presenting yourself as a person with a shepherding, pastoral heart? A political expert with the nitty-gritty on current events? A relational "mom" sharing your struggles and triumphs with other moms? A mentoring soul sharing inspiration to help others live for God?

What's your voice? And with that, what's your tone? Are you lighthearted and funny? Direct and serious? Warm and compassionate?

Voice Defines Audience

It's important to determine your voice and how you will present yourself online, as that will then determine your following, your audience. Who do you want to say this to? Who do you want to share your inspirational thoughts or political opinions with?

Do you see how this circles back to our four key development questions? Really—those four development questions will serve you well, no matter what type of writing you do!

CONTENT

What are the sources of your content? Knowing your voice and who you want to speak to will also lead to developing your content for the digital space.

When you're first starting out, it can be helpful to make a list of content possibilities. An easy example could be our writer with the book on urban gardening. Let's call her Jane.

Brainstorm for Content Ideas

Jane has decided to extend her book readership with a blog and a strong social media presence that will position her as the go-to expert on urban gardening, particularly slanted for millenials. Wise writer that she is, she first brainstorms all the possible sources of content she can use for her digital platforms.

Here's Jane's brainstormed list of possible blogs:

- Why she loves urban gardening

- The best soil types for containers

- The best plants for patio gardens

- How to build a raised bed in your backyard

- Her favorite garden hoses and accessories for urban gardening

- How to harvest your urban garden

- Optimal times for planting in containers

- Highlights from a gardening class she recently attended

- Excerpts from her book

Now that she's brainstorming, Jane's excited about the content possibilities for social media. She knows that she'll have to adjust her content for the nuances of each social media platform. And, she's researched and found that visual posts will outperform simple texts.

Here's Jane's list of content ideas for her social media platforms:

- Selfies with her urban garden

- Memes with quotes pulled from her urban gardening book

- Short how-to videos of her building a raised garden bed

- Carousel posts that reveal the steps to creating an urban garden

- Text posts with a graph to show the best times for planting

- Videos of fun times in the garden (harvesting, watering, eating!)

- Memes with tips for gardening

- Interviews with experts and friends on urban gardening

- Pics of her favorite gardening books and resources

Now that she's got a list of possibilities, Jane realizes that she'll need to have her phone handy in the garden to take pictures and record quick videos. She might even decide that upgrading her phone will help her create more visually engaging content for her social media posts.

Plan Ahead for Great Content

Jane's thinking ahead now! A trip to the local nursery turns into a live video to share on Facebook. The first apple on Jane's tree becomes an opportunity for a smiling selfie with the just-picked fruit. Jane's made a list of the best quotes from her book and she's found a site like Unsplash.com where she can get royalty-free pictures to build Facebook memes.

She's planning out her posts and building an editorial calendar so she always has something relevant and new to share as she establishes herself as the urban garden expert online. Her notes from a recent gardening symposium turn into a blog with the highlights of the event. Jane's research on a better garden hose becomes a blog with the pros and cons of vinyl over polyurethane hoses, expandable over polymer. (Did you know there were so many choices? I just googled and found an amazing article all about garden hoses!)

Jane's excited and enthused—simply because she took the time to brainstorm content that matches her online voice. She is equipped and empowered now to develop her blog and establish herself on social media.

Here's the takeaway: Defining your content now will help you think ahead. You'll plan and prepare and watch for opportunities to capture great content that will engage your followers and build your online presence.

CONSISTENCY

Consistency in voice and content will keep you on track for growth in the digital sphere. As we've seen with Jane, our urban gardening expert, your voice will affect your content choices.

In other words, if Jane's blog is all about urban gardening, a blog on the horrors of sex trafficking will seem completely out of character. Although Jane may be passionate about the topic, her readers have grown to expect gardening tips from her, not a treatise on the issue of sex trafficking. This inconsistency in voice and content can turn off or turn away her readers.

The exception may be for Jane to include a "disclaimer" asking readers to allow her to share something near and dear to her heart. Loyal readers may understand the diversion from her normal topic and stay with her; others may not.

Decide what you want to say and to whom—and be consistent with your voice and content for the best online strategy.

Keywords Can Keep You on Track

Keyword research will help you determine those few main keywords that will define your persona and topic online. If "inspirational" is a keyword included in your initial blog setup and how you've presented yourself on social media, then remain inspirational in your writing or social media post.

If faith is a keyword, then keep faith at the center. If you're the next horse-whisperer, then keywords related to horses (and their owners) will guide you in your writing. For Jane, urban gardening and those keywords associated with it help her remain focused.

Scheduling Can Keep You Consistent

Determining your scheduling frequency ahead of time will help you maintain a consistent presence online. For example, some bloggers post daily, some weekly. Choose what is manageable for you and then stick to it. Over time, your blog will become something that readers anticipate. Maintaining a consistent blog schedule will help grow and sustain your readership.

Consistency is also a vital component of a successful social media strategy. Your audience and topic will determine your best platform to build a presence on, and that platform's best practices will help establish your posting schedule. Several posts a day may be required to establish you on Twitter. Facebook may only require a post a day to keep your fans active. Again, I default to current research for what's best and what followers expect in maintaining a presence on that platform.

As you plan out your posting schedule for your blog and social media, be realistic. Always choose quality over quantity. People appreciate quality content that informs or inspires or simply makes them laugh over repetitive or drab posts that they scroll quickly past.

What is Your Online Goal?

As you develop online content, know your end goal. Ultimately, for both blogs and social media, your goal should be audience engagement. Likes, shares and comments show that you're striking a cord with your "tribe" and will help you overcome the algorithms of each platform. This translates into your posts appearing more often in people's timelines.

Converting online followers over to your website and email sign-up should be another of your priorities online. Building an author platform means cultivating fans that you can communicate with online, but also in the more consistent communication medium of an email campaign.

Make sure that your content keeps them on your website via your blog, or connects them over to your website via social media. An email sign-up and pop-up will help you capture their names and emails when they land on your website. Cultivate relationships and loyalty through an email marketing strategy. It will serve you well in the long run as you develop your writing career.

YOUR WEBSITE AND YOUR EMAIL LIST

Maybe not right away, but at some point in your writing career, you will most probably set up a website so you can ultimately build an email list. Establishing your website and an email marketing strategy to communicate with your followers will fall back on your four trusty development questions.

Answer the four development questions in relation to your web content and email campaigns, and then apply the digital writing skills we discussed in the previous chapter (which I've also included below for easy reference). I may sound like a broken record, but once again I encourage you to research current trends as far as the actual web content, SEO and content optimization, and email marketing strategies. They continually fluctuate.

For reference, here are the ten digital writing tips again:

10 TIPS FOR ONLINE WRITING

1. Keep it brief: shorter pieces and shorter paragraphs.

2. Use right-brain words for increased readership.

3. Conduct keyword research and write key-word rich content to be discovered by search engines.

4. Optimize your titles and content with your researched keywords.

5. Customize the URL to include keywords.

6. Incorporate a strong and relative call to action.

7. Structure your writing in the inverted-pyramid form for skimming.

8. Use bolds, bullets, headers and caps to maintain reader interest.

9. Add hyperlinks where appropriate.

10. Include images and videos to engage the reader.

RESOURCES FOR WRITING IN THE DIGITAL AGE

If you do a google search, you'll find a broad array of books and online resources to help you become a superstar in the digital age. Here are a few I recommend:

BOOKS

Maximize Your Influence: How to Make Digital Media Work for Your Church, Your Ministry and You by Phil Cooke. Exactly as the title describes, Phil offers an overall view of digital media that will arm you for the digital age.

Published. by Chandler Bolt. This book will help you think through the best path to establish your author platform.

Metachurch—How to Use Digital Ministry to Reach People and Make Disciples by Dave Adamson. He offers specific online strategies you can implement easily.

WEBSITES

When you're ready to set up your website, you can go two routes: hire a web designer or build your own. Although there is a lot to learn about fully optimizing a website, here are a few DIY "drag and drop" web designers to investigate and start your learning pathway to a good website.

Squarespace (now combined with Weebly), Wix and WordPress
WordPress is popular for bloggers. The drag and drop websites Wix and Squarespace also host blogs, but many people prefer the features that WordPress offers, particularly if your website is text-centric over visual.

SOCIAL MEDIA

Social Media Examiner: A great resource offering current trends and tips to keep you up-to-date on all things social.

Hootsuite: A social media planner with tons of training. **Buffer** is another popular option. Find a social media planner that works for you. Most online planners include training and education on best practices.

EMAIL MARKETING

These are two of my favorites, but there are others you can research that offer similar features:

MailChimp: An email host that offers training on best email practices.

GoDaddy: A one-stop shop to buy your blog/website domain, build a website, and develop your email campaign strategy.

EXERCISES

Depending on your current online presence, work through these exercises.

1. If you are already a blogger: evaluate your current strategy and adjust as necessary:

- Is your voice well defined? Is your content on topic?

- Do you know your audience? Who is your audience avatar? What are they searching for online that you can speak to?

- Are you utilizing good digital writing skills to optimize your content for the web?

- Are your calls to action strong and appropriate for the medium?

- Are you posting consistently?

2. If you're starting a new blog: you will need to build a website, but before you get buried in the details of building one, let's focus first on developing your voice and blog content. Answer the four development questions as they relate to your passion for starting a blog:

1. What do you want to say? What's your topic?

2. Who do you want to say it to? Who is your target audience? What type of voice or tone will best relate to them?

3. What is your medium? For this exercise, it's digital and a blog. Apply your digital writing skills.

4. What is your goal or call to action? What are your long-term intentions of the blog and the specific goal of each particular blog? Are you giving readers something to act upon or apply or ponder? Make sure you're hitting your goals.

5. How often will you post? Determine your posting schedule, whether daily or weekly.

3. If you are already on social media: evaluate your current strategy. Is it consistent with how you want to present yourself online? Does it fit with your author goals? Are you reaching your audience? Are you being social? It's never too late to make a change as you determine what your voice needs to be on social media.

4. If you don't have a social media strategy, plan one now. Apply the four development questions as it applies to your social media platforms. Think through how you want to represent yourself online:

- **Determine your voice.** Establish your overall tone.

- **Determine your content.** Be prepared to create and capture great content to share with your followers.

- **Determine your consistency.** Develop a (realistic) posting schedule in relation to the best practices of the social media platform.

Thoughtful preparation in establishing your online presence will show as you engage more and more followers. As you gain an online audience, cultivating them into an email list will help you develop a loyal following. Loyal followers will help towards a successful book launch! It all goes hand in hand.

You can't separate print from digital anymore. Your online presence is important for both.

I realize that many of my readers are screenwriters (or aspiring to it!). Screenwriting involves a whole new skill set, but in the next chapter, you'll quickly see how development will set the stage (pun intended) for a screenplay or teleplay that gets picked up and produced.

Lastly, we'll look at going further with your writing. Read on!

10

SCREENWRITING—TV, FILM AND NEW MEDIA

DEVELOP YOUR STORY FOR THE SCREEN

"The heavens declare the glory of God; the skies proclaim the work of his hands."
Psalm 19:1 NIV

What's the movie you see played out in your mind? Screenwriting is a particular category all its own, but it is a skill you can acquire. It's amazing the number of people I speak to who have a great idea for a movie but have never brought it to the page, let alone the screen.

You can do this! If God has downloaded a movie into your soul, you can learn the nuances of writing a screenplay. Or, if you've finished your book about a tremendous story, fiction or nonfiction, you can adapt it for the screen! It all comes down to adding a few new tools to your writing toolbox.

One of my favorite scripts to write was a Virtual Reality (VR) script for the Bible Society in the UK. They had a tremendous vision for using the medium of a 360° environment to share the story of creation and salvation. I was brought on as a secondary writer and developed a writing template to express the visuals that would tell this story in the unique virtual reality format.

Imagine writing the action and dialogue that happens in front of you, around you, under you and over you! There's nothing like letting your imagination soar as you embrace the 360° media. It was a privilege to share the good news of the gospel in this new medium.

I applaud the efforts of filmmakers with a vision to share their faith in this medium. I'm excited to see the rising excellence in more recently produced faith-based films and television.

No matter how big or small the screen—theater, television, computer, cell phone—every film, video or television series has an agenda, a message to promote. In one way, shape or form, the filmmakers' worldview permeates the film, which is why this is a space that Christians need to fill.

It all begins with a good script. And a good script begins in the development phase.

There are a number of excellent screenwriting books available. If you're an aspiring screenwriter or have a vision to adapt your book for the screen, I include a few recommendations within this chapter.

What I'd like to share with you are the keys to developing your screenplay along with notes on elevating your script to get it industry-ready. As a development executive with experience in film, television and new media, and a script consultant for Stage 32 (the largest online platform for screenwriters in the world with 800K members), I've read and consulted on numerous scripts and book adaptations. I will share with you the main notes I often give in my script consultations.

In other words, I'm giving you insider information! Apply these notes in the initial phases of writing your feature film script or TV pilot and you'll be ahead of the game, even as a novice.

DEVELOP THE CONCEPT

Every film or TV project has stages it will pass through before it hits the theatres or lands on a streaming platform. It begins with development, then moves to pre-production, production and post-production. You may have the idea for the next blockbuster movie, but too many screenwriters go straight to story before fully developing the concept.

Those are the screenwriters that get halfway into a script and then get stuck. Or their story begins strong but wallows in the second act. So before you become that person with an unfinished screenplay in your desk drawer or forgotten in a file on your computer, let's look at the keys to help you begin strong and actually complete your first draft.

In its simplest form, writing a good, solid screenplay—as with other writing—begins with the four writing development questions:

1. What do I want to say?

2. Who do I want to say it to?

3. What medium am I writing for?

4. What is my goal or call to action?

Let's look at how they work in the realm of writing for film or television.

WHAT DO YOU WANT TO SAY?

Remember the quote from screenwriter Micky Fisher? "A cool idea is just a cool idea." So... what do you want to say through this film or television series?

What is the theme or premise of your film? What is the worldview you are infusing into the story?

Do you want to write a good, family-friendly comedy? Great. Decide early what you want to express through that film. Otherwise, your jokes will fall flat and the comedy will rely on meaningless "wouldn't it be funny if..." thought processes, which is a lame way to bring humor into a story.

Maybe you simply want to embody "all's well that ends well." Or that a little laughter makes the difficult situations of life more bearable. What do you want to say?

Perhaps you've optioned the amazing life story of someone who overcame incredible odds. (It might even be you!) You're writing *about* their life, but... what do you want to say through the telling of it? That God is faithful and will bring you through every trial? That you can do all things, no matter how painful or hard, through Christ who strengthens you?

It's important to hash this out early in the development process of your screenplay. Knowing what you want to say will help you make the necessary choices to tell this story well for the screen. I've found this especially true when working on a project based on true events or a person's life story.

True-Life Screenplays

Most true-life stories don't present a clean narrative line or character arc. If you're writing a script based on someone else's life or your own, you'll drown in the details if you try to include every moment that seems important.

Too often, a screenwriter will feel obligated to include all the events in their attempt to "stay true to the story." We've all seen those movies that go on and on... to finally end, albeit anticlimactically. If the writer had only been more discerning with the storyline, they could have cut half the events and had a good—and probably better—story.

Defining what you want to express through this story will help you make the crucial choices of which events are pivotal to the story and which can be cut to create a clean storyline and strong narrative arc. An excellent example of a book adaptation is Christine Leunens' novel *Caging Skies*. Director Taika Waititi optioned the story, adapted it for the screen and produced the Academy Award-nominated film, *JoJo Rabbit*.

After watching the film, Leunens congratulated Waititi and commented, "My main concern was that I'd seen film adaptations so faithful to the book that they somehow ended up **unfaithful in essence**, despite the well-meaning intentions."

Choose the events and moments critical to conveying the essence of the story. If not, you'll bog down with unnecessary details and a mammoth script that no producer will touch.

The same is true for a fictional story—that comedy or drama burning in you. Determine what you want to say before you start writing and your screenplay—and ultimately the movie—will be one that audiences can follow and enjoy.

WHO DO YOU WANT TO SAY IT TO?

During the development phase, it's helpful to determine your audience early so you can write your script for that audience. Just as you consider your intended audience for a book or blog project, you also want to have your viewer in mind as you write your script.

What demographic are you aiming for? The film industry breaks audiences into four demographic quadrants: male, female, over 25, and under 25 years of age.

Are you writing for the niche of a Christian audience, or are you hoping to cross over to a general audience?

Are you hoping for a domestic release? Or are you going after an international audience with a movie that "has legs" as we say in the film industry, meaning it will "travel" and do well outside of the U.S.?

Who do you want your movie to reach?

Having an idea of the audience you are writing towards will direct story choices as well as the medium and marketing of the project. Remember that universal themes will resonate with a larger percentage of the population and translate well to international audiences.

For example, if you've ever heard the Kendrick brothers speak about their films (*War Room, Courageous, Fireproof*), you'll understand that they are specifically writing their movies for a Christian audience. They hope to offer movies that build up the church, inspiring them to live out their faith.

In contrast, the movie *I Still Believe* was produced with hopes of reaching a younger, general audience. That target audience choice affected the writing and the marketing of the film.

The large studios are always looking for a four-quadrant movie—the kind that will appeal to all four major demographics: male and female and age groups both under and over 25. However, before you announce that you've got the concept for a blockbuster film, you might consider aiming for a smaller niche—a smaller target—that you're more likely to hit, especially if you're a newer or independent filmmaker.

Write it well enough and it will create the buzz that will draw others outside your target audience. *I Can Only Imagine* is a good example of a movie produced for a Christian audience that became a breakout independent studio hit. It created such a buzz that it drew in the general public, becoming a box office success.

Now let's look at the third key development question that remarkably also applies to screenwriting.

WHAT MEDIUM ARE YOU WRITING FOR?

This question ties in deeply with the audience you are writing for. Your target audience will greatly determine the medium and where this film, television or new media project will be distributed, where it will live for viewers to watch.

Are you aiming for a theatrical release? A made-for-TV movie? Or are you hoping to land it on a streaming platform? What medium are you writing this screenplay for?

A good theatrical release still affects the overall success of a movie, but not every project is a good candidate for a theatrical. Network television; streaming platforms such as Netflix, Disney+ and Pure Flix; and the new media options of Snapchat, Tiktok, Facebook, Instagram and YouTube—are all viable platforms for filmmakers and writers to consider.

Note: The pandemic had a significant effect on theatrical releases; time will tell what the future of theatricals holds as films are often released day-and-date; in other words, the same day it premieres in the theatre, it's also available on Video on Demand (VOD) platforms.

Every medium also has unique demographics of who is watching where. The bottom line is to think about your intended audience and where they are watching and let that determine your structure choices and ultimately your medium.

WHAT IS YOUR GOAL OR CALL TO ACTION?

How do you want people to feel when they leave the movie theatre or the story ends? What is your intention? This critical decision sets the tone of your movie and thus your script or teleplay. Write towards accomplishing that feeling.

It's been said that the best movies don't require discussion at the end. It's just a good movie, and often people can't explain why—or don't need to explain why.

However, depending on the nature or subject matter of your project, you might consider adding an actual call to action. For example, if you're writing a documentary, you may genuinely hope to spur people to action. Your goal may be to raise awareness and get people behind your cause. Write towards that goal.

Recent faith-based films include a phone number or "text-to" number to connect them with study guides or even phone counselors. *I Can Only Imagine* included a call to action, offering help to people struggling with depression. Thousands responded and the movie's impact went beyond a "good film to watch" to become a movie that was literally saving lives.

Know the end goal of your film before you start writing and you'll be more guaranteed to accomplish that vision with the project.

Check Your Concept's Marketability

There is yet another step you must take your story concept through before you get too far into the project's development. As with any writing, we want our work to be read—or in this case, produced. Is there a market for your story?

You can check your concept's marketability a number of ways. When you pitch it to friends or family, does it stir interest? Are they intrigued? Test your concept by asking!

Also, take the time to research IMDb Pro and Box Office Mojo for comparables. What does this movie (or television) concept compare to concerning budget, theme and audience—and were those films successful? Why or why not?

See if you can talk to a distributor who carries similar projects. It can be invaluable to gain their input on your project before getting too far into it. They know what's selling and what's not, what audiences are drawn to and what the market is missing in meeting audience interests.

Use that information to hone your idea and pitch for the project. Maybe you've got a great concept but have the wrong audience or platform in mind. Be open to suggestions to make your story better and more marketable.

If you take the time to develop your story idea before you type "fade-in" on your script, your chances of success are dramatically increased.

SCREENWRITING TIPS

As promised, here are the notes that, as a script consultant, I find myself sharing over and over with screenwriters. Apply these notes *before* you send your script out to a producer (or send it to me for a script consult!) If you do, you will have propelled your screenwriting career light years ahead of novice, and sometimes not so novice screenwriters.

Beat It Out

To outline or not to outline? "Beat it out" means to break the story down by its plot points.

Similar to establishing a working outline for your blog or book, an outline of your screenplay will help you see holes or gaps in your story idea—weak plot points, logic holes and inconsistent characters—to help you determine if your story is solid or if you need to develop it further to truly discover the storyline.

Also, every good film will have a beginning, middle, and end with a cord running through it to keep the audience engaged throughout the film. Does that sound familiar? Bring all that you've learned to this point into the realm of your screenwriting career.

There are several ways to structure a story, but the main point is to make sure you know what good story structure is before you try to go rogue. One of the most simplified ways to approach story structure is from screenwriters Robert Ben Garant and Thomas Lennon, a prolific writing duo known for films like *Night at the Museum*, *Herbie Fully Loaded*, and *The Pacifier*.

Here's their take on traditional structure:

Act 1 – You get a likable guy up a tree.

Act 2 – You throw rocks at him.

Act 3 – You get him down out of the tree.

I've found that different stories call for different approaches, but in the end, almost every good story meets the main beats of traditional story structure. Whether you rely on conventional 3-act structure or another like Blake Snyder's Beat Sheet from his classic screenwriting book *Save the Cat* or Joseph Campbell's *The Hero's Journey*, your story has to have a strong narrative arc and meet audience expectation of the genre. An outline will help you accomplish that.

Develop Your Characters: Intention and Obstacle

As a script consultant, one of my main notes to screenwriters is to do a deep dive into their characters. Too many rely on clichés or write shallow characters with no layers or depth of insight. If you develop your characters well, your dialogue and action will be organic.

Aaron Sorkin (*The West Wing*, *Molly's Game*, *Being the Ricardos*) boils character development down to its bare bones: intention and obstacle. Somebody wants something, and something or someone is standing in the way.

What does your lead character want—and what's standing in her way? What are her motives, wants, needs and fears? What are her quirks? What makes this character unique so that an A-List actor would clamor to play the part?

Also, bear in mind that I don't necessarily need to like your lead character, but you do need to make me care about them—and care quickly. Get me invested and engaged with who they are. There's so much more to say here, but again, these are my quick notes for you to consider.

Develop Your Story World

You have one chance to suspend my disbelief and help me embrace your story world. Basically, that means you have one chance to help your audience accept and believe something other than their current reality. This is especially prominent in science fiction or fantasy genres.

Think of movies like *Avatar*, *Lord of the Rings* or *The Hunger Games*—very quickly the story world is introduced and like magic, you embrace it and are carried into the story. Establish the rules of your world early and then don't break them.

The First 10 Pages (or the first page!)

Nobody has time to read—especially in Hollywood. There are stacks and stacks of unread or half-read screenplays and your first ten pages or even the very first page could determine whether your script lands in the pile or actually gets read.

Create a page-turner from page one to two to three... and all the way through. Hit the beats of good story structure from the beginning (or at least know them before you break them!)

Every word counts, every scene counts, every character and situation has intrigue and conflict that infuses your script with drama. Apply your wordsmithing skills coupled with strong story development.

Evaluate Every Scene

Make sure that every scene moves the story along. If it doesn't, cut it or rework it. As a writer and as a director, I examine and evaluate every scene by asking myself:

1. Why is this scene important?

2. What is the emotional beat? (And has it been hit already in another scene?)

3. How does this scene serve the story? Can it be cut?

Show Don't Tell

Write visually. Paint a picture that carries the reader into the story.

Please understand that I'm not talking about set dressing—insignificant details such as a potted plant in the corner or an abundance of coasters in the living room. Let the set dressers handle that *unless* it is critical to the story or character.

For example, if the character is a neat freak, then maybe those coasters give us a clue, and insight into the character. If the plants are dead and dried up, maybe it's a sign that the character is never home, doesn't care, or is too busy to care.

When you write visually, you're opening up my imagination, not distracting me with unnecessary details. Bottom line: your narrative description should be short, visual and meaningful.

Proofread Your Script and Check Your Script Format

I read a number of scripts as a script consultant and development executive. If I see typos or inconsistent script formatting—especially on page one—it immediately signals to me that this writer didn't care enough about his story to proofread or learn proper script format.

You may have a phenomenal story, but if your formatting is off or the script is rife with spelling errors, I wonder if the rest of the story mirrors a careless attitude. Why should I spend my time reading your screenplay if you haven't made an effort to proof it or format it correctly?

If you're not a good proofreader, or if English is not your first language (I've seen that too), then get a friend to help check spelling, grammar and punctuation. If you're unsure about proper script format, google it or consult Dave Trotter's *The Screenwriter's Bible*.

Remember, you may only have one chance for someone to read your screenplay. Do everything you can to put your best work out there.

Hone Your Craft

Never stop honing your craft. I've read scripts from seasoned writers and it was quickly evident that at some point in their career, they stopped learning. Maybe they felt they had arrived, but somewhere along the way they stopped growing. Don't be that person.

Strive to get better. Stay up to date on current trends. Read the trade magazines, read the books, read Academy Award scripts. Invest in script consultations or a good script doctor who can pinpoint logic holes or fix plot problems.

If your story isn't finding a market...

- Maybe it can be better.

- Maybe it's not time.

- Maybe your industry relationships aren't in place yet.

Don't stop writing. Get your script as good as you can get it and then *move on*. Always have another project you are working on.

The film industry can be a roller-coaster ride with good news one day and the bottom falling out the next. Keep the vision of where you want to go with your screenwriting career, trust God, and keep learning and growing.

If you're serious about screenwriting, I suggest investing in screenwriting software. Some people adapt a Word document (which can be time-consuming and tedious). Others write in the free or paid version of Celtx, but the industry standard is Movie Magic and Final Draft. I prefer Final Draft and have a link for it on my website under "writing resources."

As believers, we need to fill the visual space with quality film, television and new media that will enlighten hearts with truth in entertaining ways. I pray God will guide you on your screenwriting journey and open the doors for your work to be produced.

EXERCISES

1. Do you have a movie idea? Brainstorm through the four development questions before you open Final Draft!

- What do you want to say? What is your theme or premise?

- Who do you want to say it to? Where does it land in the four audience quadrants? Male, female, under 25 or over 25?

- What medium are you writing for? Where do you envision this film or television series "living" On network TV? A theatrical release? Streaming platform?

- What is your goal or call to action? How do you want people to feel after watching your film or TV show? Is there a cause or true call to action that you might incorporate, as they did in the movie *I Can Only Imagine*?

2. Do you have a completed screenplay? Apply the notes within this chapter to elevate your script and become an expert at writing in this visual medium.

The saying that writing is re-writing really applies in the film and television industry. Don't be content with your first draft. Keep elevating your script until it's the best you can get it. Then set it aside for a month and take a fresh look. You'll be amazed at how you can elevate it further before sending it out to a producer.

Last note: if you're interested in a script consultation, reach out to me on my website under "script consultations."

And now, let's finish things out with one last chapter...

11

GO FURTHER—REPURPOSE AND WRITE MORE

EXTEND YOUR STORY

"The words of the godly are a life-giving fountain..."
Proverbs 10:11 NLT

We're at the end of the book, but the beginning of your journey as a writer! You may have begun this book with the seed of an idea for your writing project. Hopefully, you've moved past barriers, maybe moved a few mountains or two to establish the practice of writing daily, and now that seed of an idea is a close-at-hand reality for you.

You have the tools in your hand now to write anything you want.

A book

A blog

A screenplay

A song, a play, a short story or web article.

The principles are the same. Armed with the four key development questions and a writing process from idea to outline to finished draft—you are a writer.

Take a minute and let that thought settle in. You're no longer dreaming; you've begun the path that will allow you to write compelling content that will engage audiences. You are well on your way to becoming a writer who can turn hearts and minds towards truth or a new perspective. You know the steps you need to take to write whatever is on your heart—and to write it in a way that people will grab hold of.

As long as you continue to jump the hurdles that might bar your way, you're going to do it. You're going to publish your book or start your blog. You're going to write that screenplay. I can feel it. I know it—as long as you keep to the path.

Before we close, I want to add one more tool to your toolbox—one more weapon to your writing arsenal.

REPURPOSE YOUR CONTENT

I do this every single day—repurposing my content—and you will too as you write. Repurposing means taking a body of writing, say your book, and finding ways to repackage it for other mediums or extend the story to reach a greater audience.

Remember my story about the article I wrote for FamilyChristian.com? "Safe – The High Tower of the Lord" was the all-time highest performing article on their website at the time (and it may still be). It touched tens of thousands of lives and I thought, "How can I reach more people with this content?"

It was a timely article, written at the beginning of the pandemic when so many people were dealing with uncertainties and the shaking up of all things "normal." The concept of God as our safe place struck a chord in many people's lives. So I considered and brainstormed: How can I repurpose the article for another medium and/or another platform to extend its reach? How can I increase the impact of the truth and hope it conveyed?

From that brainstorming session, I developed the article into a 3-day YouVersion devotional for their Bible app titled "Safe: The High Tower of the Lord—3 Days to Re-Center During Uncertain Times." Then, I reached out to a friend who translated the devotional into Spanish.

Next, I revised the 3-day devotional for the iDisciple platform and it now lives on iDisciple.com as a growth plan. Additionally, I've developed graphics and social media posts from the content of the initial article.

It's hard to track the total reach of my repurposed content, but a safe estimate is that *at least* another 60,000 people were blessed and encouraged. Do you see the potential?

Smart Writers Repurpose Content

Reach isn't necessarily the only reason to repurpose your content. Part of it is just being a resourceful writer. You don't have to reinvent the wheel. For example, let's say you've finished your book. It's going to print and you've celebrated the glorious moment.

Now it's time to put on your smart cap and consider: How can I repurpose this content?

You are holding a gold mine in your hands! Gold nuggets of content that can be reworked for other mediums or platforms:

- Blog posts culled from your book chapters

- Lead generators (free downloadable whitepapers) developed from bullet points within a chapter that will help you build your email list

- Social media posts

- Memes with endorser quotes or your own "power quotes" within the book

- A press release announcing the book with copy from your back cover or pulled quotes from you, the author

- Web content about the book for your landing page

- Articles and op-eds you can send out to media outlets

- Talking points for your interviews as requests come rolling in...

The list goes on and on! You don't have to start from scratch. You don't have to rewrite everything. Repackage your book's content, revising as necessary for other mediums or platforms. See what I mean about a gold mine—a wealth of content you've already worked hard to produce?

Repurpose Your Fiction Work

You can repurpose your fiction work as well. Your script turns into a novel, or vice-versa, your novel is adapted for the screen. Or a dramatized podcast. Perhaps a storyline within your non-fiction works turns into a short story or is condensed for a magazine like Reader's Digest.

It's simply a matter of learning another medium's nuances or "rules" and reworking your content for it. Remember our third development question?

What medium am I writing for? This is where you consider the medium and adjust your original content to fit. Extend your reach and impact by repackaging your content in a new way.

Build a Super Story

Another way to repurpose your content is by extending the story to reach a new audience. In this case, you're not just reworking content but building upon the original story and spinning it off into multiple platforms and mediums.

A great example is Marvel Comics' *The Avengers*. Consider how many spinoffs exist! Captain America, the Hulk, Spider-Man, the Black Panther, the Black Widow, Iron Man—the list goes on and on!

They've taken the original Avenger story, extended the storylines, created new ones, and then branched out into various forms of media and an array of platforms. You may not get a twenty-something female to read an Avenger comic book, but you can get her into the theatres to watch the movie! By creating what my friend Houston Howard, author of the book *You're Gonna Need a Bigger Story* terms "super story," Marvel Comics greatly expanded their audience. (I highly recommend his book as a resource at some point in your career.)

Brainstorm Your Super Story

Consider the novel you're working on. Can you extend the story of one of your characters to create something new? Perhaps there is an interesting supporting character that you might explore further. You could write a whole new novel based on that character's life.

Or, if you've written a book about marriage, perhaps you can spin this into a subsequent book about parenting. Jane's book on urban gardening gets a sequel about raising chickens in an urban setting. If you start thinking in terms of "super story," you'll have a lineup of books or novels waiting to be written and read by an ever-expanding audience.

Another well-known example out of Hollywood is the *Breaking Bad* television series written by Vince Gilligan. (It deals with tough topics, but it was brilliantly written.) One of the supporting characters within the series was a lawyer called Saul. After *Breaking Bad* finished its run, Gilligan wrote a new TV series further exploring Saul's storyline—thus extending the original story. *Better Call Saul* found an audience and has seen multiple successful seasons.

Another way to extend your story would be to consider a sequel to your original novel or television series. We see it when hit movies get spun into television series. Author Lee Child's *Jack Reacher* is an excellent example of something that began as a novel and was developed into a feature film. The storyline is now being extended through a television series of the same name.

Another example of an author who extended their story beyond the original is J. R.R. Tolkien. His twelve-volume series expanded the books *The Lord of the Rings* and *The Silmarillion* to explore further storylines and characters. His classic *The Lord of the Rings* was developed into a feature film series, and now the story is further extended with a new television series. The TV series explores the legends of Tolkien's created Middle-earth, taking viewers into the history thousands of years before the setting of the novel, thus extending the story.

Extending your story may take some serious brainstorming, but it's yet another way to 1) capitalize on the hard work you've already put into your project and

2) reach more people in a whole new demographic. The number of lives you can reach is incredible if you're smart about this. And, guess what? You already know how to do this.

Creating a super story based on your original work rests on asking yourself the four key development questions for this spin-off or extension. Imagine Tolkien as he considered extending the story of *The Lord of the Rings*. Talk about development! He created fantastic story worlds and characters, and you can do the same.

What characters in your novel lend towards further exploration? What topics in your book could be expanded upon?

Open your writing toolbox and develop the idea. Make sure you choose a pathway that will appeal to your existing audience or a new one. Consider the medium that will best serve this expanded storyline. And think through your goal or call to action throughout.

Repurposing your content and exploring options to extend your storyline are strategies to reach a greater audience. A skilled writer (that's you) can persuade people toward new ways of thinking and living by using multiple mediums and platforms to share your work.

Cover the Earth with God's Glory

This brings me back to one of my favorite scriptures and one of my main goals in writing this book: to inspire you on your writing journey.

> "The earth will be filled with the knowl-
> edge of the glory of the Lord as the waters
> cover the sea." (Habakkuk 2:14)

This is a given! It will happen! The earth will be covered with God's glory as the waters cover the sea. Imagine it.

Now, what we don't know for sure is your level of participation in this grand plan of God. But here's what's important for you to realize: your book or blog may seem minuscule. It may seem of little effect—but it is a drop of rain and every drop of rain counts towards covering the earth with God's glory.

And, if you're a *very* smart writer, you'll think of ways to repurpose that content. Your "drop of rain" could turn into a river, adding to God's glory and reaching more people than you can imagine.

Reaching people with truth. Encouraging them with light. Inspiring them with hope.

Your words matter. Your faith matters. My prayer for you is that you will take all you've learned in this book and apply it. Put it to work and fulfill the dream in your heart.

NEXT STEPS

What's next? Take a risk. Send your writing out to someone. Submit an article to a magazine and see if they'll pick it up. Attend writing conferences to help you hone your craft and connect you with other writers and opportunities.

Believe in yourself *and* in the gifts and callings God has placed upon your life. You'll know you're a writer when you don't feel satisfied unless you're writing.

Writers write—and they dream and think and pray! Push the limits off yourself and amazing things can happen.

You can do this. *You* can write.

Acknowledgements

I realize I am the sum total of what others have poured into my life. To that end, I give my thanks to...

My husband, Samuel A. Woodworth. Thank you for the gift of my first Macbook so many years ago, and for believing in me and spurring me on.

My kids, David Woodworth, Sarah Schultz, Esther Wasson and Febe Chiarelli (and your families). Thank you for being my "silver bullet" of support and sounding board in all my creative endeavors. My special thanks to Sarah Schultz who offered her notes to elevate this book and make it shine.

My friends, Randy and Sherry Long, who believed enough in this book and it's message to help make it possible. I pray this will be a light to help you write your own beautiful stories.

My Jesus—my Lord, my Savior and my God. He is the Source of all my writing.

I am forever grateful.

About Laura Woodworth

 An award winning writer-producer-director, script consultant, writing coach, and development executive for Cooke Media Group in Los Angeles, Laura's passion is Jesus and her goal is to inspire others to live lives that display God's glory and goodness. With a B.A. in Ministerial Studies, graduate work in UCLA's Professional Program in Producing, and currently pursuing her Master's degree at Asbury University, her awards include the International Christian Film Festival's "Most Inspirational Short Film" and the Telly award-winning documentary *Asia: The Great Wall and Beyond* produced for TBN.

A contributor to FamilyChristian.com, iDisciple and Pure Flix Insider, Laura's YouVersion devotional plans have over 220,000 subscribers. Her new devotional *Through the Valley—Move Your Life Forward in God* published by Family Christian Publishing gained #1 New Release for Religious Faith on Amazon it's first week, and her new book, *Write Above the Noise—Key Concepts to Develop Your Best Writing* released summer 2023. Laura and her husband Sam have four amazing kids and five equally amazing grandchildren. With a background in full-time ministry and missions, Sam and Laura are still on a mission to cover the earth with God's glory.

Find out more at LauraWoodworth.com.

ALSO FROM LAURA WOODWORTH

Do you ever feel like there is something more to life? Deep down inside, you sense something new and exciting is just around the corner—if you could only move past your grief or recover your momentum.

Through the Valley—Move Your Life Forward in God is the compassionate hand-up or the friendly "push" forward that will help you step into the promising future God has for you.

Find out more at ThroughTheValleyDevotional.com (or scan the QR code).

Free Gifts for Writers

I've designed several free resources to help you continue to grow spiritually and professionally, including:

- **3 Steps to Build Your Content Development Strategy**

- **Enter In – A Guided Prayer to Draw Near to God**

- **Bible Verses for Christian Writers**

- **7 Steps to Making Wise Decisions**

Access them all at LauraWoodworth.com/free-download or scan the QR code below.

It's my free gift to you!

ARE YOU READY TO ELEVATE YOUR BOOK OR SCRIPT?

Whether you're working on a book, feature film script or television pilot, you can elevate your project with a professional consultation. Additionally, if you're in the conceptual stages of a project, a consultation can guide you through the process.

Editorial consultations include a manuscript read plus a 60-minute phone or Zoom call to share notes on concept, plot and character development, story world as well as structure and organization as it applies to fiction or non-fiction writing.

- **If you're writing a memoir**, an editorial consultation offers the opportunity to explore ways to convey your story in the most engaging and impactful way! We'll discuss strengths of your project as well as pinpoint ways to elevate your work with an eye to the current industry and marketability.

Script consultations include a script read plus a 60-minute phone or Zoom call to share verbal notes on concept, genre, character development, dialogue, set up of story world and structure. You'll also receive feedback on the marketability of your script plus have opportunity to ask questions and gain my input as a working industry executive.

If you're interested, contact me on my website at LauraWoodworth.com/script-consultations. Mention this book and receive a "friends and family" discount of 10%.

Writing Coaching: From time to time I have writing coaching openings. Contact me at LauraWoodworth.com if you'd like to apply.

THANK YOU FOR READING MY BOOK!

If you've found this book helpful, I'd be extremely grateful if you'd take a few minutes to write a review on Amazon.

When you post a review, it makes a huge difference to help new readers find the book and start their writing journey.

Were you inspired or motivated? Did it take your writing and development skills up a notch? Be authentic and simply let people know how it's helped you.

Thank you!

—Laura Woodworth

P.S. I'd love to hear from you. Send me a note when you publish your first book, start your blog, or finish your screenplay! Connect with me on my website at LauraWoodworth.com